Hot Property
Easy Home Staging to Sell Your House
for More Money in Any Market
—Alexandra Newman

WILEY

John Wiley & Sons Canada, Ltd.

The Material in this publication is provided for information purposes only. Laws, regulations, and procedures are constantly changing, and th examples given are intended to be general guidelines only. This book is sold with the understanding that neither the author nor the publisher is engaged in rendering professional advice. It is strongly recommended that legal, accounting, tax, financial, insurance, and other advice or assistance be obtained before acting on any information contained in this book. If such advice or other assistance is required, the personal services of a competent professional should be sought.

Library and Archives Canada Cataloguing in Publication Data

Newman, Alexandra

Hot property : easy home staging to sell your house for more money in any market : a Canadian guide / Alexandra Newman.

ISBN 978-0-470-15316-1

1. House selling. I. Title.

HD1379.N43 2007   643'.12   C2007-902560-9

Production Credits

Cover design: Ian Koo
Interior text design: Michael Chan
Front cover photo: Tomasz Majcherczyk
Printer: Quebecor—Taunton

John Wiley & Sons Canada, Ltd.
6045 Freemont Blvd.
Mississauga, Ontario
L5R 4J3

Printed and bound in United States of America

1 2 3 4 5 QW 11 10 09 08 07

TABLE OF CONTENTS

PART III: The Processes

Appendix

The Stagers

ACKNOWLEDGEMENTS

Without all the great stagers I got to know, this book wouldn't have been possible. So Heather, Jenn, Shona, Bruno, Allison, Joy, Cesare, Julia, Nora and Paula—a big thank you!

A special thanks to Tomasz Majcherczyk, who made himself available to take wonderful photos at short notice.

And finally, thanks to my family for tolerating all the declutter, purge, display and rearranging "experiments" I put them through while writing this book.

INTRODUCTION *Your World is Now a Stage*

The prospect of selling my house has always made my blood run cold—not the sale part of it so much as the hard work of packing and moving. That's why I haven't moved for 12 years, even though I frequently feel the urge to pull up stakes and find a new house that will better suit me and my family.

In my business—design writer and lifestyle TV researcher and producer—I see a lot of houses, so the temptation to get something "better" is ever present. Although not a home stager, I understand the desire to move. And the desire to maximize this investment. According to a Royal LePage poll a few years ago, three-quarters of Canadians have a strong attachment to their homes, yet move from those same homes on average every seven years.

What gives? Simply this: our needs and those of our families change and often we outgrow our current space.

So how did this non–home stager come to write a book on the subject? I did what I do best: ask a lot of questions of people who are professional—and

passionate—about their work. And I drew from my 15-plus years' writing in the area.

The first thing I did was ask myself: What is it readers most need to know about how to get a home ready to sell? What will help them sell their homes successfully, quickly, and for the best price?

First, it's important to think about the way we regard our homes, and to acknowledge how much they mean to us. Most stagers will tell you that when you sell your home, you need to think about it in unemotional terms, as "your biggest investment" or "just bricks and mortar." But if you've lived in your house for any time at all, you have accumulated memories—most of them good, I hope, and some not so good—and those are hard to tear yourself apart from. Even when memories are bad (if you're selling your house because of divorce or a death, for instance), it can be difficult to be detached about the selling process. Home represents so much more than bricks and mortar—it's an inextricable element of our life story.

I prefer to look at home staging as a way to reveal your home's best features, a process by which you can convey to the world why this home has brought you so much pleasure. Loving your home makes it difficult to let go of—but ironically, it also makes it easier for you to sell. After all, when you believe in what you're selling, it's a whole lot easier to convince other people of its merits.

It's this love for your home—and its potential for friends and family to connect and be happy—that you want to draw out and show to the world of prospective buyers. Because isn't that what we're all hoping a new house will do for us—make us happy? Happiness at home, of course, comes in different expressions for different people—perhaps it means a layout that will nurture the family's togetherness, or a space that's more conducive to entertaining, or a home office that's comfortable and relaxed but also professional. Our homes should also be respite from the frenzy of our workaholic ways and our urban speed. They should make us feel *happy*. Forget what you hear about the latest colours and clean-lined interiors—most of us want warmth, comfort, an oasis. Think of the dozens of open houses you've gone to—what stood out? Probably the homes that made you want to sit down and stop for a moment.

What makes you happy—a home that handles all the departments of our busy lives, a kitchen you can cook in, a bedroom you can finally go to sleep in, *with little or no maintenance*? Hold that thought, and carry it into your own home staging efforts.

In order to write this book, I had to put myself in the shoes of someone about to sell their house. I went through my own house with an eye to what would be needed before I could put it up for sale. I tested out a lot of the ideas—decluttering, cleaning, purging, creating better storage, fixing things that were broken, adding things that would facilitate better function for my family.

My hope for those who read this book is that the tools here will not only prepare you to sell your house—quickly, and at the best possible price—but will help you create a better and more functional home, wherever that may be.

PART 1 *The Design Basics of Home Staging*

CHAPTER 1
GETTING READY *Psyching Yourself Up to Sell*

So, you think you want to sell your home. Or maybe you need to sell—for a new job, a new relationship, a larger family, a smaller family. No matter what your reasons, selling your house makes for a stressful time of getting your house in tip-top shape and then keeping it that way, even while you carry on with your everyday life.

What to do? Well, you've picked up this book and that's a start. By giving you solid design info, sound real estate advice, and the inspiration and courage to conquer new heights with Do-It-Yourself design, this book should make the process as stress-free as possible.

What is staging exactly?

Staging, fluffing, or dressing is the process by which you present your house in the best possible light to prospective buyers. This is done by paring down, editing and streamlining what isn't working in your interior, and by reorganizing or showcasing what is. Staging ensures that the buyer's eye is drawn to the positive features of a home. This might involve a simple rearrangement of what you have or it might be as complex as renting furniture, accessories and art.

What staging is not, however, is the process of concealing and defrauding with a pretty "lipstick-and-mascara" plan. For one thing, going to such "creative" lengths is unethical. For another, a house inspection will find it out. Finally, it's unnecessary: Toronto real estate agent Joy Verde recently sold a staged house for $250K over asking, *with the disclosure that the basement was leaking!*

Why bother to stage your home?

As one stager quipped about the real estate market, "The times, they are a-changing." Already we're seeing signs of a market in some distress—in the United States it's crumbling, with thousands of foreclosures, mortgage bank stocks plummeting and prices stagnating. Even with Canada's strong resource-based economy, we're starting to feel the slowdown, in spite of the occasional hot months.

That means buyers have more choice and it also means that you, as a seller, need every competitive advantage.

If you've picked up this book, you probably already recognise the value of home staging.

A home is often the largest investment you make in your lifetime. When it comes time to sell, you want the best return on your investment. But it's hard to analyze your own home's strengths and weaknesses, assess the target market, and then prepare your home for presentation. Successful home marketing requires a unique set of skills that will catch the eye, and imagination, of the potential buyer—a buyer who has high expectations, fed by a slew of shelter magazines, home décor television shows, and subdivision model homes.

You've probably heard many anecdotes of home staging successes. And the stats back them up: when Coldwell Banker Realty (US) tracked sales records on almost 3,000 properties, ranging in price from $200K to almost $5M, it discovered that while the average home was on the market for about 31 days, staged homes usually sold in about 14 days. It also found that the average home sold for 1.6% over the seller's asking price, while staged homes went for about 6.3% more than asking.

Certainly, the returns outweigh the costs. HomeGain, an online resource for homebuyers and sellers, found in a 2003 poll of 2,000 real estate agents that staging costs anywhere "from $212 to $1,089 and adds from $2,275 to $2,841 to a home's selling price—a return of from two to 13 times the cost of staging."

If you're moving up to accommodate a growing family, why not get the most out of your existing home so you can get the most house for your money? The same goes for downsizing—get the most for your home to ensure the most for retirement.

As for success, this is what the stagers tell me:

"An agent called me to stage a house that had been listed eight months before but without staging, in spite of the agent stressing the importance of it. The new buyers decided to sell, and they called me to stage it. Just eight months later, in a market that was starting to soften, the house fetched $58K more than it sold for the first-time around without staging."

"Last night the little bitty condo we staged listed at $259K, had five offers and sold for $288K, with an investment of $7K and one week of labour."

"I was sitting on my dock last summer when a client called, and asked if I was sitting down. The house they'd spent $17K staging had sold the night before with multiple offers for $550K over asking!"

You may think your home is tidy and up to date—in fact, a 2005 Royal LePage poll found that 75% of Canadians think the same. But home stagers have a different story—they find that *everyone* is a packrat and almost all homes need at least a little decorating help.

Thankfully, it often doesn't take much to tweak a house into saleable condition. Most stagers would agree that paint gives the highest return for a small investment, with lighting and flooring not far behind. Sparkling clean windows and spotless kitchens and baths are equally important.

The empty house syndrome

Another reason to stage is to enhance an empty house. Whether it's been flipped or the owner's new job has prompted an immediate location change, that empty house is a challenge: people have a hard time imagining it as their home. That's because buyers fall in love with an overall feel—a feel that is hard to create without furniture, carpets, art or accessories. This is especially true with condos, where small spaces have buyers scrambling to figure out how their furniture will fit.

How much, and what's involved?

How long staging takes and how much money you spend depends on a lot of factors, such as the size and state of your home, how much work you can do yourself, and the selling price. In a million-

dollar neighbourhood, you'll need to ratchet up the bells and whistles more than you would in an area where homes sell for $300K or less.

If you bought your house ten years ago for $179K, have done few repairs in the meantime, and want to list for $600K, be prepared to do some work. Jennifer Brouwer, who staged the suburban home shown in Part Two of the book, says that people should be prepared to spend up to 10% of the expected selling price to really maximize their sale. If they bought a long time ago, and have invested little in it, that percentage could be more. For example, when she and business partner Shona Fitzgerald staged an empty million-dollar monster home out in the country, it required $40K in furniture rentals alone.

"We do our research," Brouwer says. "We check out the neighbourhood's prices to figure out where to draw the line. We'll ask what the client bought it for. If you bought last year at top price, but you're getting divorced and need out fast, your staging design plan will be different than if you bought 10 years ago, have time on your hands and stand to make a large profit."

How long does it take?

Brouwer says that if you have furniture and accessories and all that's needed is editing and rearranging—and no painting—staging can be done in as little as a day. "Often, we get calls from real estate agents who want to put a house on the market right away, and if there's enough to work with, we can get it ready in a couple of days." If there's little or nothing in the house, it could take a week—to rent furniture, temporarily install drapes, paint—and if there's any renovation involved, it can take a month or more, Brouwer says.

Then there are the houses like the one in the suburbs that Brouwer and Fitzgerald staged. Owned by a man who spent most of his time at his girlfriend's, the house had become a landing strip for 12 years' worth of clothes, paperwork, receipts, and old furniture. It cost $1,800 for three Dumpster loads and because the home had not been maintained, they needed to redo floors, reface cabinets, change countertops, rent new furniture and get new window treatments. Though the seller was reluctant to move when he saw how wonderful his home had become, he was thrilled to get over asking when the house was listed at the top end of the neighbourhood's price point. Without those changes, it would have listed for about $200K less, and probably would have sat for months. (See transformation in Part Two.)

The process can take anywhere from one day for minor tweaking to three or four weeks, depending on the size of house and state of property. What's crucial is what state the house is in. If painting, repairs, renovations, finishing floors are needed, then time required is longer. If the owner hasn't decluttered for some time, then time is required to sort through and store, donate or dispose.

What staging should accomplish

1. Get a better price for your home than if you hadn't staged.
2. Fix glaringly bad problems.
3. Create better flow.
4. Create functional, comfortable, attractive areas that allow you (or any prospective buyer) to prepare and eat food (with family and friends), relax, lounge and gather.
5. Create rooms that have identifiable functions, or functional identities—a dining room for eating, a living room for gathering, a bedroom for sleeping or retiring, a bathroom for cleansing and rejuvenating, a home office for working.
6. Create environments that are conducive to making you feel good. With a typically hectic life, most people just want to feel happy at home. If you can create an environment that telegraphs this, you've got a winner.

Overall steps to success

The following chapters go into greater detail on how to stage a home yourself for maximum profit, but the basic must-do's are as follows:

Clean: Sounds obvious, but Glen Pelosi, contributing designer of the popular television series *Take This House and Sell It*, says it's the single biggest impediment to selling a house—and he's seen a lot of dirty houses.

Purge: Packrats of the world unite—you have *everything* to lose! A quick look inside anyone's closets confirms we all have way too much stuff. When buyers open crammed closets, their first impression is that the house is too small for their own stuff to fit.

Declutter: Differs from purging in that you will edit your possessions. Those two sofas and the club chairs your family loves to sink into? They may be *très* comfy for you guys, but they make the living room feel stuffed, so something's gotta give. Too much furniture, art and objects is like being overweight, so put your rooms on a diet to slim them down to be airy and spacious.

Focus: Create one for each room—a fireplace, view or great piece of art in the living room, a china cabinet, beautifully dressed table or mirror over the buffet in the dining room, a sumptuous bed. Buyers want clear direction on how the house should be used—rooms with too many functions look sloppy and confusing.

Light: It's an elusive mistress, especially in our northern climate, so seek ways to bring as much of it as possible into your rooms.

Smell: It's too important to overlook. Artificial scents can overpower and trigger allergies, so stick to natural—flowers or fresh baking.

Balance: Seek moderation in all things— especially in colour. If your furnishings are strong colours, but in good shape, update the walls in neutrals. If furniture is pale, coloured walls will make them pop out.

Arrange: Edit your art and accessories, arrange according to style or room colour, and display in groups of 3, 5 or 7 (not 10 or 20!).

Now that you have the broad brushstrokes of what it takes to prepare your home for sale, are you ready for the next steps? Read on.

CHAPTER 2
TAKING STOCK *What are the options?*

Do I leave or do I stay?

The process of selling a house is a challenging one. Before committing to it, do some serious soul-searching—are you sure you want or need to sell? Are you selling for the right reasons? Some situations don't allow for other options: you may be moving across the country to take a new job, or perhaps your marriage has ended and the divorce agreement requires that the house be sold. In those cases, you still want to get the best price from the sale of your house, and staging will be an important step in the process.

But maybe you're thinking of selling because you've heard about friends making $300K. (Yes, it happens!) Or you believe the market is softening so it might be best to cash out now. All markets are relative, though, and you still need a place to live. A move up will cost you hot market prices, in addition to high real estate fees, moving expenses, and so on. Downsizing to cash out will be the same, unless you plan to move to a considerably lower-priced region, city or neighbourhood.

Some agents suggest that you have at least 25% equity in your home before selling—this way you don't need to take out a second mortgage or insure the first through Canada Mortgage and Housing Corp. (CMHC).

Another reason to sell may be that you lack space in your current house. As most clutter experts will tell you, however, it's not usually the house that's the problem, it's the stuff and the packrats who live there. Home stagers say that the major portion of their job is decluttering (a topic covered fully in Chapter 3), and that once rooms are clear, there's suddenly a remarkable amount of space. It's just part of the human condition: we all crave space, but once we get it, we proceed to fill it.

Sometimes reconfiguring space is all that's needed to make your current house the home you really want. Designer Anna Simone (of Cecconi

Simone Interior Design) once told me that it may not be a question of lacking space, but of a poor layout. She and partner Elaine Cecconi worked with one client who was convinced of the need for an addition. After analyzing the space, the better solution proved to be removing the wall between the kitchen and the unused dining room, and purchasing furniture that was more practical. "It solved the space crunch, improved the home's overall flow, and cost a lot less money, time and energy," Simone says.

Before spending money—or moving—she suggests analyzing how you want your environment to work for you, writing down what you use the rooms for, how often you use them, what works and what doesn't. (Incidentally, this works when you're looking to buy your next house, too!)

For a relatively small consulting fee, a trustworthy and experienced contractor can assess the challenges and give a rough cost estimate for the renovations you'd need if you wanted to tailor the home to your needs. That way, you can accurately weigh the pros and cons of moving versus staying and renovating.

Sometimes a move will bring you closer to what's important: friends, the dog-walking park, a community of worship or the schools your children attend.

Perhaps you're on a busy street and you have toddlers; maybe the neighbourhood doesn't feel as safe as you'd like, or the schools are a little dodgy.

Perhaps your kids are at university or with families of their own, so your five-bedroom house is more than you want, and a little condo downtown sounds perfect.

Perhaps your little house in the city has a big mortgage and you'd like to make the budget easier to balance, and so you're thinking of downsizing by moving out to the burbs. Worse things could happen! All good reasons, but think long and hard about the potential disadvantages. Nothing is perfect, after all, and while life in the suburbs might grant you a bigger house, the cost of gas and the long commute times might be more taxing to your lifestyle than the extra square footage is worth.

Before moving, look carefully at your financial situation (how much can you really afford every month?), how a move will affect your lifestyle and what the market conditions are (for example, are homes selling easily? is it a volatile and unpredictable market?).

Whatever the reasons, make sure you and your partner are on the same page. According to a 2006 Gallup poll reported in *USA Today*, "spending too much [money] and saving too little" conspires more than anything to tear couples apart. If one of you fancies a home in a pricier neighbourhood and the other is more cautious about adding to the debt load, the discrepancy in your values can lead to serious relationship problems.

Looking honestly at your home

Let's assume that your deliberations are done and everyone is in agreement that it's time to sell your house. First, put on your glasses.

I hate housework so much that the best way to avoid it is not to wear my glasses around the house. While I'm not so blind I trip over things, my eyesight is just fuzzy enough to blur all signs of clutter, dust bunnies and fingerprints. And, that's how most of us go around our houses—we just don't see the flaws.

For example, a friend of mine, gearing up to sell her house, replaced the kitchen floor and ceiling but left the fridge in its spot on the insulated back porch. When I told her it would seem weird to potential buyers, she replied, wide-eyed: "But it works really well for me." She's become so accustomed to pulling things out of the fridge and placing them on the ledge nearby that she has forgotten how unusual this is.

Most of us adapt and forget. We'll walk through the dining room because the piano blocks the front hall, or work a complicated series of elastics on the bathroom door because the lock is broken. But to potential buyers—in the six to ten minutes they're in your house—these things are extremely annoying. *Even if they do the same kinds of things at their own home, they don't want to pay for your quirks.*

Sit down with pen and paper and list your home's attributes, the things that made you fall in love with it in the first place. Was it the wonderful entry hall? The proportions of the rooms? The ensuite bathroom? The fireplace? Write down anything you've done to enhance those features, and list any other improvements you've made to the house, inside and out. At what point did the house work perfectly for you, and at what point did you outgrow it?

Now list the flaws—why you're moving, why the house no longer works for you, what needs fixing, what drives you crazy. This exercise, done thoroughly and in detail, will provide a clear blueprint of what needs doing before you sell your house. Stagers call it a "deficiency list," and it includes things such as cabinet doors sticking, switch plates missing, and so on.

After you've done an inventory of your home's attributes and deficiencies, it's time to be more objective. How do other people see your home, and how does it stack up against other houses in your neighbourhood? To get an outsider's view, you might ask a few friends over for drinks and/or dinner and give them a questionnaire to fill out about your house. But ask them not to sign their names—you value friendship over honesty, no?

Now check out the competition—such as open houses in the area, or model homes—to see what they have to offer, and how they market themselves for sale. The features that are consistently emphasized will give you an idea of what the buying demographic is looking for in your neighbourhood. In neighbourhoods that attract young

Example:

ROOM	REPAIR	EDIT	REMAIN	STAGE
Front Hall	· Hardwood badly damaged—either replace or refinish; alternatively could paint in diamond pattern on the bias	· Threadbare runner removed · Remove rickety shoe rack · Remove most of the coats inside the closet, and declutter closet shelves	· Pretty hall bench	· Add small mat just inside front door · Piece of landscape art
Living room	· Slipcover the old cat-scratched sofa · Paint walls	· Remove curtains, extra chair, coffee table and both end tables · Declutter bookshelves beside fireplace · Remove half the art	· Sofa · One chair · A few choice pieces of art · Sisal rug	· Rent or borrow a large new coffee table · New drapery panels (Home Depot?) · Layout is cluttered, furniture needs to be rearranged
Bathroom	· Repair leaky toilet · Install glass front étagère over toilet · Replace towel rack	· Throw out half the medicine, makeup and toiletries	· Fixtures · Beautiful Sea Island basket collection	· New towels and bath mat · New shower curtain · New soaps, candles, small wicker basket to hold toiletries at sink

families, for instance, you'll notice an emphasis on space (number of bedrooms, size of back yard) and proximity to schools, parks and shopping. Listing the pros and cons of your neighbourhood will help you highlight the best things, and also help you narrow down the demographic looking in the area. When you know who is most likely to be interested in your home, you can market to them more effectively. Your real estate agent should also be able to help you with this.

Note prices in your neighbourhood and what you get for the money. If laminate counters reign supreme, for instance, then installing granite will be a wasted indulgence. Take note of any creative alternatives that you see, such as a charcoal-grey laminate countertop trimmed with cherrywood bullnosing. Identify those things in other people's houses that make you feel good, and not so good.

Describe your home—as it is right now—in 30 words for an imaginary real estate brochure, imagining yourself as a potential buyer. Be honest! From what you've written, ask yourself if you'd want to buy this house for top dollar. After you're finished staging, you should be able to honestly write 30 words that would have you desperate to buy it.

Who'll buy my home?

There's no way you can make your house desirable to absolutely everyone who walks through the door, but apparently there are some characteristics that almost everyone is looking for. When *Better Homes and Gardens* created a dream home based on the responses of 60,000 readers, they came up with a list of the most frequently cited components of the "dream." People repeatedly said they wanted the following: a feeling of space and a sense of light and air (the more natural light in a room, the better); connection to the outdoors through materials such as limestone, slate, etc.; low maintenance; and anything that facilitates laid-back, easy living, but which can be dressed up a little for entertaining.

How people make buying decisions

Real estate surveys suggest that curb appeal is nine-tenths of the selling law.

This view seems to be supported by Malcolm Gladwell, social theorist and author of *Blink*, a book "about the kind of thinking that happens in a blink of an eye." Gladwell says that the mind only takes a few seconds to jump to a conclusion but one that's based on a "perfectly rational" thought process. In other words, when all the cues and clues are there, the rational mind will make an informed, but fast, assessment of your home.

To guide buyers toward a positive first judgment, ensure the front of your home is clean and well maintained.

As designer Nora Lukss says, "Buying a new home represents so many things to a buyer: a new beginning, a better beginning, the culmination of a dream, an expression of one's success (that is, wealth)."

"Merchandising" at home

Paco Underhill has been researching how people shop for more than 30 years, and has published two books on the topic, *Call of the Mall* and *Why We Buy: The Science of Shopping*. Here's what he's found:

- Our culture is extremely product savvy. (Lesson for home stagers: a few well-placed name brand products can make a big impression.)
- The longer a shopper remains in a store, the more they buy; amount of time spent in a store depends on how comfortable the experience is. (Lesson: make them comfortable.)
- All shoppers must cross a zone of transition: whatever's just inside the door won't get noticed, but move it in 10 feet and it will be. The law of nature is that shoppers need a landing strip; customers get frustrated with wandering and when the layout is confusing. (Lesson: rooms with clearly identified functions, plus unimpeded traffic and circulation routes, win the day.)
- People slow down when they see reflective surfaces. (Lesson: mirrors make us stop and take our time; too many, however, are overwhelming.)
- People look immediately to the right when entering a space. (Lesson: establish an atmosphere of light, warmth and colour in the front hall, with flowers on a table, or a bench.)
- "Address seating," says Underhill, before anything else. "Air, food, water, shelter, seating, in that order. Before money. Before love. Seating." (Lesson: make all seating beckon and invite buyers to sit; arrange the most comfortable seat where it takes advantage of a good view.)
- People will buy from someone who cares. (Lesson: provide info that people can read and take away with them, such as a brochure with detailed specifications about the house, renovations and repairs, etc.)
- "Shopping is female…pay attention to how women wish to live, what they want and need. Even the enormous changes in the lives of men and children are merely in response to the lead taken by women." (Lesson: highlight the way a house looks and feels, plus the efficiency of the kitchen, the amount of clean play space, and a spot for her to retreat.)
- Cool isn't necessarily better: one finding was that a marble-floored Hallmark store brought lower sales than Hallmark's more traditional outlets. (Lesson: people want warm and familiar rather than cool and trendy.)
- Shopping habits are changing, and much shopping is done online. (Lesson: good photos on the MLS sites are crucial.)
- Shopping is more about display than selection. (Lesson: display goes a long way to create a positive shopping experience.)
- In a touch-deprived society, we want tactile experiences when we shop. Underhill says touching, hearing, smelling or tasting accounts for almost all unplanned buying in a store, and claims that possession begins *when the shopper's senses start to latch onto the object. It begins in the eyes and then moves to the touch.* (Lesson: if buyers like what they see, and feel drawn to touching, they're already feeling a little ownership.)

When to call an agent

In any market, a house needs to be priced properly *from the start*. A beautifully renovated and staged house up the street from me was listed at $699K a year ago, in a fairly strong real estate market. But it was $100K too high. Although they've since dropped the price by $110K, it's still sitting. Why? Because it's stale—when nobody touched it at the original price, buyers grew suspicious that something was wrong.

Stagers and agents are divided on whether to call the agent before or after you've staged the house (see Chapter 14 for more on agents). Some say the agent's feedback from the beginning can set you on the right path, while others say the first (bad or otherwise) impression sticks forever, even with an agent.

My advice would be to clean and pare down, and attend to small repairs (since you'll have to anyway), then call in the agent to find out what features to emphasize. The agent will know best what the market in your area seeks. In a family area, for instance, three bedrooms are a must, but in a primarily single or childless couple area, the third bedroom could safely be turned into an office. That rule, however, is also made to be broken. When Nora Lukss listed her multi-level house in a family-oriented neighbourhood, the first agent advised creating three bedrooms, but the house didn't sell. The second agent suggested emphasizing the home's best features and turning one of the bedrooms back into the office it once was. Along with other changes, the house sold in a few days of relisting. (See transformation in Part Two.)

CHAPTER 3
THE PURGE *Have Less, Sell for More*

Roll up your sleeves and get ready for step one— you're about to purge your life.

From packaged foods bearing prehistoric best-before dates, to last decade's (or last century's, last millennium's) clothing, to mismatched glasses and dishes, it will go and you will feel better for it—a weight (literally) off your back. It's said that we use only 20% of the items we have in a home—and those five iron skillets in the bottom of my pot cupboard are proof of this.

It's hard to part with things—in fact, most organizers will tell you their work is not about closets, but about personalities and the reasons we're addicted to our *stuff*. As British designer Terence Conran writes in *Small Spaces*, "Good home organization is more than shoe racks and shelving…it involves a fairly radical reappraisal of all our belongings and the manner in which they are used and stored. [It] goes to the heart of why we acquired things and more importantly why we continue to hang onto them. The fact that we are

fortunate to have this problem at all, and that we enjoy such a degree of affluence that getting rid of things is more of an issue than getting hold of them in the first place, in no way takes the sting out of the situation."

American designer Alexandra Stoddard, writing in *The Decoration of Houses*, says that people are "hopelessly nostalgic… we cling to memories of the past." Her take on clutter is that editing is important, even if it's just to "liberate yourself from the stuff—and to make it easier to move." She recommends learning how to "edit the good from the bad, the relevant from the irrelevant, the treasured memories from the dated items." Get rid of what's ugly or not used, she advises: "No item should be depressing, no matter how necessary."

The great 19th-century British designer William Morris coined a memorable and helpful maxim: "Have nothing in your homes that you do not know to be useful, or believe to be beautiful." In

Below: There are so many toiletries in this small bathroom. There's precious little room to use them! Nobody wants to see a jumble of half full bottles, so put them all away. The result? Pure zen and a feeling of space.

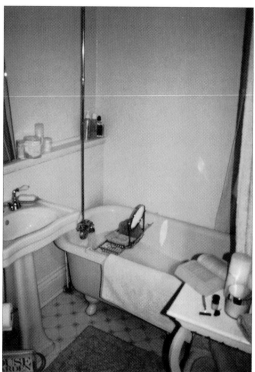

Photos by Alex Newman

other words, have only what you love, or what is useful to you.

Start with a clearly defined focus and tackle one room at a time. Designate three containers for garbage, storage and giving away—and be ruthless. Michael Corbett, author of *Find It, Fix It, Flip It!*, advises that you remove everything from the space, and put it in the garage for 48 hours, then re-introduce some items. "You are going to hate it," he says, but by the next day it will start to look more normal. "And by day two, when you try to put all the items back, you won't be happy. It will feel too crowded. Congratulations! You have just learned how to edit. You are on your way."

Ideally you should start this process as much as a year before listing, but a couple of weeks of really focused effort should be enough to whittle the stuff down.

Most people seem to develop a kind of paralysis when it comes to sorting out their things, and it helps to have someone point out what to do. Living with all those things makes you blind to the need to get rid of anything. One stager told me that a client whose children were grown and gone felt she had to upsize in order to fit her furniture—in particular a dining suite that she never used!

Questions to ask and quick tips to help you decide what goes:

· Does it fit—your style, your body or your taste? Try clothes on in front of a full-length mirror—better yet, in a three-way mirror—because seeing is believing. Keep only what fits, is in style and needs no alteration or repair. You might also discover an ensemble you'd have overlooked in your previously full closet. Toss or give away any clothing you would not want to be caught wearing if you: a) died; b) had to go to the hospital; c) ran into an old high school chum; or d) had a chance meeting with your boss outside of work.

· Is it past its best-before date? Examples are yeast packets (for that French baguette you've been meaning to bake), pectin (for those preserves you're on the verge of making) and old medications (consult with your pharmacist before disposing medications).

· Is it being used? Did you even know you had it?

On one recent hunt, I found eight containers of my husband's deodorant. Consider tossing old nail polish, VHS tapes (if you no longer have a VCR), cassette decks, record players (unless you're an audiophile); and pots and pans you never even take out of the cupboard (most pot sets, by the way, are a waste of money, since at least two of the pans never get used—you're better off buying individual pots).

· Would you give it a second glance if you were out shopping right now? If not, toss it.

· Does it make you feel guilty that you never read/made/used/fixed it? Think of all those "home handy gal" projects in the basement. I have a needlepoint pillow I've been working on for 25 years, a wicker carriage purchased 20 years ago that still needs painting and a wrought iron bed frame purchased 18 years ago that is still without the side rails.

· Old receipts can be recycled. For tax purposes, keep receipts that are 7 years old or less.

· Other paper items can go too: magazines, newspapers, clippings of old stories (I've had one story I've hauled around for more than 20 years, convinced I'll use it somehow but never have), recipes you haven't looked at, expired insurance policies, bank statements, coupons, etc.

· Get rid of overstocked items. If you've got 10 jumbo packs of paper towels, 10 new bottles of shampoo and so on, see if the store will take them back for a credit.

· Put away all political or religious mementoes, since you don't know who will be coming through your house, and you don't want to turn off anyone who might find either your religious or political affiliations offensive.

· Remember that simply hiding stuff in your basement or garage doesn't work—people investigate those spaces too. You'll have to use your best storage and organization practices to keep those areas from looking cluttered and overburdened.

Getting rid of it

Consider charities such as the Salvation Army or Goodwill, or local women's shelters or nursing homes. Some charities will even pick up large items. You might have friends who want some of your stuff. If you have things to sell, hold a garage sale, or try craigslist or eBay (if time is short, however, these may not be viable options). Consignment shops may be a good alternative, since you can move things out of your home immediately and not worry about how long they take to sell.

The importance of having storage

All buyers value space, especially storage space. In fact, it's a major reason that people move. A 2005 Royal LePage poll found that "the top three interior features when selling a home were freshly painted walls (30%), flooring (29%) and organized storage space (20%)." Although storage is ranked third as a feature, when the same poll asked how important storage space was to a potential buyer, 86% ranked it as seven or more out of ten, suggesting storage is a major issue. This is especially true for women: compared to 32% of males, 54% of women ranked storage space as the most important thing in a house.

Experts agree that a minimum of 20% of your living space should be allotted for storage. That may sound like a lot, but when you think of the things we store—seasonal items such as skis, toboggans, bikes and decorations, papers for the home office and taxes, paint, tools—that space can be taken up fast. The rule of thumb for storing is: keep frequently used items close by, sometimes-used items in a fairly accessible location, and anything else (seasonal or occasionally used items) in storage. While you're selling your house, off-site storage is best, so consider the options of friends, family, or commercial storage facilities in your area.

Commercial storage is more sophisticated now than ever: you don't have to settle for an unheated garage-style space somewhere out in an industrial mall (although that's still the least expensive option). Store Your Style (www.storeyourstyle.com) is a Toronto storage facility that comes right to your house, with rolling clothes rail, wooden hangers and breathable, gusseted garment bags. You sort through your wardrobe, select what you need for the season, and store the rest away with them.

Some furniture storage companies also offer door-to-door service. Toronto Storage Stadium (www.storagestadium.com) will come to your door and handle the packing and care of stuff you otherwise might have to permanently unload. You can fill their large crates on your own, or pay an hourly fee for two workers to do it for you.

Working with the storage space you have

If you don't have the time, or seem to be unable to declutter any more than the bare minimum, you should consider calling in an expert. Closet organizing specialists will not only look at clothes closets, but also kitchen cupboards, pantry areas, laundry rooms, garages, basements, tiny closets, dining areas, living rooms and bathrooms to find space where you need it.

If you're going to take a stab at reorganizing your storage spaces yourself, the first rule is to make sure that your closets are clean and uncluttered. Take everything out, repaint or clean the closet itself, then re-hang only those items that you use or wear regularly. Purge as you go.

Now for some room-by-room storage specifics.

Bedrooms

Professional closet organizing companies offer closet storage systems that are fantastic—but can also be quite expensive. A cheaper alternative is the builder's store DIY closet kits that give you double rods, hanging shelves and even drawers.

Plan ahead by measuring your current closet and figuring out hanging requirements and storage needs. As you clear everything out to install the new system, go through items and purge. Double closet rods—one over the other—are the best way to squeeze more storage space out of a closet. Be sure to measure the clothes you'll be hanging there and allow another six inches of clearance above and below each rod. With deep closets, install shelves on side and back walls so that you can see and access everything, rather than lose sight of it all on a 30-inch-deep row of shelves.

Add soft-sided cubby storage, which is simple to attach and makes good use of the closet space you have, to house folded items. Upper wire shelves are perfect for out-of-season items stored in clear bins with lids. To streamline the look of your closet, invest in hangers that are all the same, either plastic or wood.

If your closet is also your dressing area, make it more functional by hanging a large mirror on a wall or door. Floor-length mirrors are preferable, especially for women.

If some or all of these ideas are beyond the scope of your time or budget, at least keep your closets scrupulously neat and tidy. And fold your sweaters!

Living room

The most obvious place to find living room storage is in armoires or entertainment units, although these bulky items can make a room appear smaller, especially in an already small room. Built-ins are much better, but if time and budget are tight in prepping your house for sale, then pick up storage options from a builder's store or IKEA and, if time permits, add moulding so it looks built in. Low chests of drawers acting as end tables are also great storage.

Another option is wall shelving, either cantilevered (attached on one side only, and without visible support) or with brackets. When painted to match the walls, these shelves recede visually. Shelving is best if it takes up a whole wall, or an alcove, rather than intermittent shelves placed hither and yon. They should be tailored to what's stored on them: larger and heavier items are better on lower shelves, for instance. A group of floating shelves can be installed over the credenza to display photos and books.

Kitchen

Recycling and garbage storage needs to be tucked out of sight, preferably under the porch or deck if it's easy to access. These are areas that men like to investigate thoroughly. According to shopping guru Paco Underhill, women are more interested in what goes on inside a home, while men take an interest in things that go on outside a home. Stager Heather Shaw agrees. She believes that if you let a couple loose inside a house for sale, the woman would head for the kitchen and bedrooms, while the man would head down to the furnace room, out to the barbecue grill, or for a look-see under the deck.

One of the most important things in a kitchen is to keep the counters clear: buyers want to know they'll have ample room to prepare food. Michael Corbett (author of *Find It, Fix It, Flip It!*) suggests organizing food cabinets by like items, putting together all the cereal boxes, cans, coffees, etc., and then "directionalizing" them, the way they do at a grocery store. While that sounds a little obsessive-compulsive to me, he's the flipping expert, so he should know! That said, it does look neat and tidy to have matching storage containers. Buy a number of the same type of container and label each one for a unified appearance.

Laundry room

Don't forget this often overlooked room. Wire shelves suspended above the washer and dryer will keep cleaning supplies at hand. Better yet, an off the shelf kitchen cabinet stores laundry essentials nicely.

Hallways

In your entry hall, wicker baskets on the top shelf of your hall coat closet will help contain the typical tangle of mitts, hats and scarves.

In your hall linen closet, use dividers on shelves to keep stacks of sheets and towels from toppling over and getting tangled. (Available through Lillian Vernon, www.lillianvernon.com.) If you don't have a linen closet, try stacking linens in a glass-front cabinet. Tied with ribbons makes them pretty.

Bathrooms

As with the kitchen, the key thing to remember about the bathroom is to keep countertops clear. Keep your everyday items, such as toothbrushes and toothpaste, in a medicine cabinet or drawer if possible. Use clear plastic storage containers to corral infrequently used items such as manicure tools or medications, and stack them neatly under the vanity. A multi-pocket vinyl shoe bag is another idea if you have a full-height closet in the bathroom: hung from the inside of the door, it will hold lots of toiletries and keep your essentials handy and visible. Check out www.containerstore.com for storage options.

CHAPTER 4
THE GROUNDWORK *Repair and Clean*

After the first purge, it's time to tackle repairs.

Stager Kelly Fallis identifies the work that must be done by tradespeople right from the start. "Decisions are made according to budget and discussed by us with the Realtor and homeowners. If there are many repairs to be done to the house and budget is an issue, then we try to choose the most important from a buyer's perspective. If a buyer can see that there is just a little to be done to the house, we are ahead of the game. They can then plan for some renovations and justify the cost in their minds."

Finding Mr. Right

No, I'm not talking romance, I'm talking service. Mr. Right is a guy who will fix your home from top to bottom, and take his bad table manners home with him at the end of the day.

What you're looking for are small repairs—those things we never get around to, such as paint chipping on the door trim, cracking floor tiles, or the hairline fractures in the shower grout.

After the first cleaning, you'll also be able to see the state of the paint on the walls. If they aren't squeaky clean and bright, you'll need to paint. (For advice on colour, see Chapter 6.)

Replace faulty or dated handles on all doors. When Heather Shaw took me through a house she was preparing to stage, one of the first things she noticed was the mismatched bedroom door handles—easy enough to fix. The same goes for outlet and light switch plates—clean and/or replace, but make sure they all match up in colour, material and style.

Patch nail holes in plaster or drywall with a ready-to-use plaster compound or spackling, and holes in wood (trim, doors, windows, etc.) with wood filler. Wipe off excess immediately so it doesn't dry in a rough patch.

Glue peeling wallpaper, or consider repapering or stripping completely and painting fresh. Make sure cupboard doors open and close properly—most of the time, it's just a small matter of tightening a screw in the mechanism. Fix dripping taps by replacing washers.

If a few vinyl tiles on your kitchen floor are loose but the floor is otherwise in fairly good shape, replace or re-attach individual tiles—apply tile glue to the underside, press down firmly, weight down with a heavy object and let dry 24 hours.

Fix all tile grout. It seems like a small thing, but grey, mildewed, or cracked grout shows up like a beacon in the night.

If your hardwood floor is dinged in a couple of spots, use wood putty to smooth it out, wipe excess and let dry 24 hours. You can also use wood stain markers or finish pencils for scratches.

Now for the White Glove Squad

There are agencies that do deep cleaning for homes being listed. But if you're doing it yourself, start by getting down on your hands and knees and crawling around your house. You'll soon see where the dirt really is: at the bottom of the kitchen cupboard kick-plate, on baseboards and in the cracks of the floors. Then look up to the top of doors and windows. While buyers are not likely to crawl around on your floors, the overall cleanliness contributes immeasurably to a home feeling solid and well cared for.

Yes, I mean really clean

Cleaning, in this scenario, doesn't mean just washing down walls. It means going to obsessive lengths:

using an electric toothbrush to clean inside crevices, such as where the kitchen sink meets the counter, the hardwood meets the baseboard or another type of flooring, the handles meet the oven or fridge door, and even in the faucet base, hardware grooves, the inner edge of the dishwasher panel, the oven window. Paintbrushes do a great job of dusting hard-to-reach spots, like door and window frames, light fixtures and anything with deep engraving.

The hidden nooks and crannies of your home are well worth your time and energy. When Heather Shaw stages a home, she pays close attention to the furnace room and the electrical panels. In one house she recommended they replace the electrical panel: "The wiring had all been replaced and was up to date," she says, "but the electrical panel looked awful and that screams 'danger' to a potential buyer."

She also maintains that there must be clear and free access to the furnace and hot water heater—she even washes them down or vacuums them. "If your furnace is new but 45 cans of paint are stacked in the furnace room preventing someone from getting close to it, that suggests it hasn't been touched for a very long time."

Windows

A vacuum attachment will get into the grooves of windows and screens; afterward, clean with old rags, dishwashing liquid, or vinegar and water. Open the windows and let the fresh air in—it will help with air circulation, and will clear away any lingering pet, food, or cigarette odours.

Shake drapes out, dust thoroughly, then vacuum with the attachment about an inch away from fabric. To remove small spots, try baby powder on a toothbrush. If all else fails and they're still grimy, send to the cleaners. Vacuum sealed wooden blinds, then wash with a mild soap solution or vinegar and water.

Walls

For grimy walls, mix a few spoonfuls of dishwashing liquid, window cleaner, or liquid clothes detergent in a bottle of water, spray on walls and let rest, then wipe with a damp sponge. And Magic Clean truly is magic for removing resistant dirt, such as fingerprints and newsprint smudges (right next to your husband's reading chair).

Furniture

Vacuum not just carpets but the tops and arms of upholstered furniture. If this doesn't refresh your furniture, mix two caps of Woolite in a bucket of cool water, and sponge gently onto backs, seat cushions and pillows. If they're still not fresher, consider professional steam-cleaning. If that doesn't do the trick, store elsewhere, give away or buy a pre-made slipcover.

Rubber gloves dipped in water and rubbed along furniture will remove pet hair. Masking tape rolled around your hand, sticky side out, also works.

Lampshades

To clean lampshades, place the shade in a tub of Woolite and water solution and roll it gently from side to side, using a sponge to make sure the surface is moistened. Clean inside of shade. Blot dry with a colour-fast towel; make sure it's dry, since water drops leave marks. For silk lampshades, professionally clean only.

Rugs and carpets

For deep cleaning rugs, turn topside down on a clean sheet and vacuum the bottom, then turn over and vacuum the top. With a damp sponge, gently rub any dirty or stained areas, then brush pile with a soft carpet brush.

If the carpet is ivory, though, you may need to haul it onto the deck for a thorough scrubbing with soap and water and hose it down—or have it professionally steam cleaned.

To remove wax, place wax paper on top, cover with a tea towel and apply a hot iron—the wax will come up.

Appliances

Vacuum or use a bottlebrush to clean fridge coils (you find these by flipping up or removing the grille on the front at the bottom of the fridge).

Appliances should be spotless—undiluted vinegar does the trick on stainless steel, and microfibre cloths work wonders with just water. WD40 or nail polish remover will remove gummy sticker residue (such as the energy seal) from white appliances, including the furnace, hot water heater, washer and dryer. Make sure to clean floor and wall vents as well.

Loose wires

Bundle wires from the computer, TV and gaming equipment so that they're not a messy tangle. Twist ties will bind individual wires.

Bathrooms

Squeegees clean shower doors, tile walls and windows exceptionally well. Pick one up in the automotive department of a hardware store where they're cheaper.

Grout will come up white if you use a soft scrub brush and one of the following: bleach, vinegar or CLR. Automotive wax brings back the lustre of a porcelain bathtub.

Kitchen

Counters, fixtures, sinks and faucets should be free of waterspots. Don't forget to dust the plumbing under a pedestal sink.

Clean your microwave by heating a mug filled with water and lemon slices. Let the mug sit for a few minutes after the timer goes off—the baked-in spills lift off and the lemon gives a fresh scent.

An open box of baking soda left in your fridge removes odours; baking soda mixed with warm water is also great for cleaning the fridge interior.

Clean the range hood filter by running it through a short cycle in the bottom of the dishwasher.

If you display silver, make it shine with toothpaste, but choose one of the less abrasive brands, since toothpaste can scratch.

Hardwood floors and wood cabinetry

Tennis balls remove black scuff marks on hardwood floors when they are rubbed over the marks. Orange oil will renew the original lustre to wood cabinets that have become dry.

Smells

Fabric softener sheets or unwrapped soap bars placed on your closet shelves keep them smelling fresh. Or make sachets out of dried lavender or rosemary and mint.

The worst offenders are pet smells. No matter how scrupulously clean you are, pets do smell. According to Royal LePage's 2005 poll, this negatively affected sales more than any other single factor! Your best bet is to house your pets elsewhere while the house is listed. If you can't bear to do this, then you have a few other options. First the litter box must be out of sight—hide it inside the bathroom sink cupboard with the doors removed and a curtain to allow kitty access. Make sure you've had the carpet and furniture professionally steam cleaned to remove odours. Ask a neighbour to come in for a whiff test. Put away pet food and water bowls. Put away their toys.

If you're a smoker, consider giving it up or smoke outside until the house sells. Stale smoke is easily detected by buyers, especially non-smoking ones. Have drapes and carpets and upholstery professionally steam cleaned to eliminate the odour and thoroughly wash walls and ceilings—or better still, paint—since smoke residue clings.

Outdoors

Depending on the type of exterior you have, you may be able to use a power-washer to get it looking clean. Concentrate on are cleaning the windows, soffits and siding. If you're going to power-wash the exterior brick, you must take care that the power-washer is within the 500–1000 psi range—it'll state it on the box or the machine—anything over 1500 psi risks damaging both bricks and mortar. You can rent power-washers by the hour or the day, but I bought one for about $150 and use it all the time. It also cleans deck boards really well so they look new.

CHAPTER 5
LAYOUT *Making Sense of It All*

We have a funny relationship with our space—we long for open space and yet we also crave coziness. When it comes to selling your home, err on the side of spaciousness. Scale, proportion and proper room and furniture layout will help you achieve this.

British designer Terence Conran, in his book *Small Spaces,* makes a distinction between "coziness and claustrophobic." He explains that a too-open space "can be as uneasy in its effect as one that is excessively confining. A large, open space can make you feel small, which is not a very agreeable feeling at all. Coziness on the other hand implies a quality of ease and rightness, of a space that is scaled to equalize human needs and limitations."

Gathering and retreat

As Marco Pasanella notes in *Living in Style Without Losing Your Mind*, homes are divided roughly into two general areas: gathering and retreat, or public and private space.

Gathering places are most inviting when they're uncrowded, filled with soft, textural furniture, appealing and warm neutral colours, and the inviting sounds of music, water or a crackling fire. Gathering often happens around food—in the dining room, the kitchen, even around a large coffee table.

Retreat spaces are those spots for getting away—a study, bedroom or bathroom. Spaces for retreat don't have to be big as long as they're comfortable: a window seat or a comfy chair, a small table and lamp; a terrycloth-covered stool and tub tray for doing your nails; dozens of pillows, a book and a cozy throw in the bedroom.

Flow

Flow is the way space moves—or the way space allows people to move in and through it. When the flow is good, a room feels larger, because there is nothing obstructing movement, either in the physical or visual sense.

Circulation space is what helps you move through a house—stairs, halls, corridors, landings. When these spaces are clear and uncluttered, it makes travel from one spot to another easier, improves flow and sense of harmony, and gives the illusion of more floor space. In fact, 19th-century Arts and Crafts architect Sir Edwin Lutyens was so convinced of the value of "wasted" space in creating the illusion of spaciousness that he incorporated wide stairways and halls into his house designs, at the expense of adjoining rooms.

If you have made a long-range home staging plan, and it will increase your asking price (check with your agent first), consider partially or fully removing an interior wall for better circulation, such as the wall between a narrow hall and a small living room. Raising door heights and widening doors helps by providing better views into each room, so that the rooms feel more visually connected. Both of these projects, however, do require the advice of a reliable contractor, and may require building permits from your municipality. At the very least, consider taking some of the interior doors off their hinges.

Even in an open concept space, you need clearly marked circulation routes. These help guide you into and through distinct areas: a runner in front of the entry can lead you to the kitchen, a sofa and chair grouped on an area rug signals a living room, and a table beside a wall with art and semi-concealed by a lattice screen indicates a dining area. The "paths"—however you want to devise them—that lead toward these rooms are the circulation routes.

Good flow can also be created through the use of colour, either a continuous wall colour from room to room, or in an accent colour carried through each space by accessories, furnishings, art, rugs. In open concept spaces, a continuous wall colour expands the space, but colour blocking on one wall or two in a deeper tone of the same colour will add interest and emphasis.

Space plans

Buyers want to see clearly identifiable and functional spaces. Develop a space plan by first determining the area demographic. For example, the single buyer will be more interested in a second-floor den/home office than a third bedroom.

Determine how well the house functions by covering the basics:

1. places to gather: for conversation, for TV watching, for food prep and for eating
2. places to retreat: bedrooms for sleeping; a bath for soaking, cleansing, facials; a nook to read in

It doesn't matter that you have a big living room, a den *and* a family room as much as there's somewhere to entertain, lounge, read and watch TV in a comfortable and reasonably stylish way, without intruding on the privacy of others who are doing something else.

FLOORED!

What's underfoot is often overlooked, but for creating cohesion and good flow, nothing works quite as well as floors. While frequent transitions in flooring render an interior choppy and make it feel small, consistent flooring smoothes out the transitions from one space to another. You hardly notice the change, for instance, when ceramic tile in the entry is in the same tonal family as the hardwood or carpeting elsewhere.

Hardwood

Durable hardwood is, hands down, the most popular flooring choice, especially in the principal rooms. The more you have of it—exposed or even hidden under carpets—the better for selling. So if the floors are beautiful, uncover them, and where time and budget permit, sand and restain them. When floors aren't in good enough shape to finish—and if your house is in a high-priced location—consider installing new floors at least on the main level, and carpet on the second level.

Keep in mind, though, that you can do a relatively quick sand-and-refinish of your floors as long as you don't plan to change the colour by adding stain. Staining, on the other hand, requires sanding down to completely bare wood, since any finish left on the surface will keep stain from penetrating and you'll end up with an uneven application of colour. In either case, it's a big job that involves moving everything out of the rooms where the floors are being done, and you'll want to use lots of plastic to seal off those rooms. Even so, the sawdust will likely reach other rooms.

Carpets and rugs

Area rugs add colour, texture, pattern and definition to any room. A bright kilim can infuse a neutral modern room with warmth and vitality.

In open concept homes, area rugs define the various spaces, direct traffic flow and pull together conversation areas. Rugs also help muffle noise levels. In empty houses that have been staged with minimal furniture, they can help to compensate for the echo.

Generally speaking, a loose, all-over pattern in a rug helps to open up a room. A large floral Oriental should only be in a large room. Dense geometrics and tight patterns help enclose a space, which can be a good thing if you're trying to pull in a conversation seating area.

Rugs should leave three feet of floor exposed all around the room (so, in a 12-foot by 12-foot room, use a 9-foot by 9-foot rug). For a really pulled-together look, and if you can afford a large enough rug, place furniture on the rug rather than on its edge.

To tone down a formal setting, add a casual rug such as seagrass or sisal, or plain textured wool. To dress up a casual shabby-chic living room, and create a little movement, add an Aubusson (floral tapestry).

Wall-to-wall carpeting that's seen better days may improve with a shampooing, but if it's really dated or in bad shape, it's well worth the money to redo. Invest in good underpadding—buyers usually are wearing only socks on their feet when they tour a house and a plush carpet underfoot, especially in a basement, is a pleasure they won't likely forget. This applies to replacement carpet only, because if the basement is unfinished, and possibly damp, throwing down a new carpet will only mask a deeper problem.

Tiles

The sky's the limit on tiles—there's ceramic or natural stone, 6-inch square up to 24-inch square, and the colours of the rainbow available. There's any number of creative things you can do with the tiles, as well—for example, laid on the diagonal, they can visually widen a narrow room. 12-inch by 12-inch squares can be customized by cutting into numerous sizes, such as 6-inch by 12-inch or 2-inch by 2-inch, and using the various pieces for a unique pattern.

Pulling up old tiles is a messy thankless job—you're better to work around the tiles you have if possible than to try and do a new tiling job, at least for staging. What Jennifer Brouwer and

Photos by Tomasz Majcherczyk

Shona Fitzgerald did when faced with the two 1980s-era bathrooms (one pink, the other grey) in the suburban house they staged (see Part Two for this transformation), was to keep the tiles and change fixtures where possible—tub, toilet, sink, faucets—and paint walls a neutralizing cream colour. Replacing the tiles would have added another two weeks onto the job—and a significantly higher invoice.

Other materials

Sealed cork has been popular in Europe for ages, and is finally catching on in North America. When varnished and sealed, the tiles are impervious to moisture, and require virtually no maintenance. If damaged, tiles are easily replaced.

Linoleum is another great floor—and it's back in style, partly because it's environmentally sound, made of burlap, canvas or felt, mixed with linseed oil. Don't try to paint over it, regardless of what some diehard do-it-yourselfers say—it's a messy job and the paint chips easily.

A new product called Tech Stone is a granite look-alike that you can apply over tiles, linoleum, and even outside on the deck. A mixture of ground stone and acrylic, it can be easily applied in three steps. (See Resources at the back of the book.)

Subfloor

Sometimes when you strip off the linoleum tile or vinyl sheet floor in your old kitchen, you'll find a pine or fir subfloor. If you think the kitchen would work with that rustic or whitewashed cottage look—and the flooring isn't so rough that you'll get splinters from it—then sand it down and paint the subfloor—it will add brightness and a casual atmosphere. You can also paint a diamond pattern of two alternating colours quite easily.

If your hall floor has seen better days and there's either no time or money to sand and restain, then consider painting it. Use a fresh, trendy colour (but remember the continuous flooring palette rule), or a diamond pattern.

Noise is one of the biggest challenges in today's open concept homes, so having areas that are set apart from TV noise, but which remain connected visually, are in high demand.

Individual room layouts

For each room, develop a floor plan, using the following questions to guide you:

1. What's the focal point? Each room needs one, so if there isn't one now, create one. For example, a living room fireplace, a dining room table or buffet, and the bed in a bedroom are all focal points; furniture should be arranged to guide the eye to the room's focal point.

2. What is the room used for? This will dictate what furniture to use. If the room multi-tasks, stick with no more than two functions and make clear what these are—for example, in the dining room, a table and chairs and an armoire with concealed home office workspace; OR table and chairs, bookcases and a big leather reading chair; OR table and chairs, piano and bench accessorized with a brass music stand and a thick rug, but not all four functions of dining, reading, music and home office. (Just on the piano—although many families have one in the dining room, if that's a small space, store the piano off-site.)

3. What's the traffic flow like: Is it easy to move in and through this room? When you move through the room will it interrupt others engaged in activities? In living rooms where reading, watching TV and talking requires sitting, the need to move isn't as great, so focus your efforts on furniture groupings.

4. Are there architectural features to highlight? If you have high baseboards, crown mouldings, nice windows, etc., the object is to uncover them and show them off!

5. Are there nooks and crannies that can be turned into vignettes? A small extra room on the main floor becomes a snug little den when outfitted with a leather sofa, ottoman, area rug and TV, and the landing in the upstairs hall becomes a home office area with a writing desk and armless chair (if it is very small, it's best to leave open).

Try out the floor plan on graph paper, if you have trouble visualizing. Using a scale of one-quarter inch to one foot of real space, accurately draw each room, showing available wall space, and the positions of doors, windows and built-ins. Then place your furniture on the graph paper, using proportional paper cut-outs that can be moved around. Alternatively, take photos of the rooms, make black-and-white photocopies, and play around with colour and arrangement. For a really easy view of your house, Home Hardware has a new easy to use software program called HomeWorks, which promises to demonstrate rooms with various colour and furniture arrangements.

Focal point

Create a focal point. A room's focal point—fireplace, cabinet, piece of art, picture window—should be anchored against a wall, to design the furniture layout around that. But don't line furniture against the walls like soldiers, unless the space is so tight you can't avoid it.

In a living room with two focal points, arrange furniture in such a way that the largest piece can take advantage of both: the sofa beside the fireplace and opposite the picture window, for example. If there's no obvious focal point, create one out of the room's function. For example, a living room with neither a view nor a fireplace could have a beautiful antique armoire as a focal point. Keep the backdrop simple and the colour palette consistent.

If the room is on the long and narrow side, break it into two areas—one around the focal point, and a secondary seating area in a vignette comprising two chairs and a side table. Use area rugs to anchor furniture arrangements, define space and add colour and texture.

In a bedroom the focus should always be on the bed—the more sumptuous the better. This is especially important in a small bedroom, since there's room for little else. Consider angling the bed from a corner, making it even more of a focal point. Add a steamer trunk or baskets at the foot of the bed for emphasis.

Room function

While it's tempting to change rooms around in order to provide something you think a buyer might like, it's generally better to return a room to its intended use while the house is being listed.

Sometimes flipping rooms makes more sense. Think about which rooms get used the most and why—is it the furniture, or the layout, or where it falls in the traffic pattern?

When Julia and Cesare staged the small detached house (pictured on the following page), they felt the living and dining rooms needed to be flipped because the living room would be the space immediately visible from the entry. The bonus was that the existing wall colours worked better with the newly switched-around rooms; the green sofa and maroon chair blended better with the green walls of the former dining room, while the pine table and chairs and folk-painted blue hutch stood out in the yellow room.

Although having different living room and dining room wall colours worked well for Julia and Cesare, a continuous colour palette through the main floor is usually easier to work with. You can more easily switch furniture around, which maximizes your options for space function. A continuous wall colour also creates a unified look throughout the home.

Although most stagers will tell you not to double up functions in a room, some rules are meant to be broken. An artist friend of mine has a library and dining room combination that multi-tasks in the most beautiful way, with book-lined walls, brass sconces, a table with six chairs and a Venetian wall mural.

Traffic patterns

Know your traffic patterns before moving furniture around. There are a few general rules for traffic: allow three feet for pathways in and out of a room;

Tomasz Majcherczyk

Tomasz Majcherczyk

chairs and sofas should be no more than eight feet apart (anything more makes conversation difficult); and allow 18 inches between sofa and coffee table.

Each seat should have a table or some surface—about the same height as the chair arm—for books and refreshments and there should be a lamp to read by. When staging, though, keep in mind that those extra tables may be too cluttered, so prepare to move one or two out.

Move furniture away from walls as much as possible, rather than pushing sofas and chairs right against the walls. Pulling the furniture in has the effect of making the conversation area feel more intimate. As well, people like to look out windows when they're house shopping, so make sure no furniture will prevent them from doing so.

Furniture placement

Making a furniture plan for an entire house is easy! Just list all your furniture, see what you need and what you don't in order to demonstrate the function of each room by starting with the anchor pieces (seating, tables). Fill in the colours, and arrange the accessories. All right, maybe it's not exactly easy, but it is doable if you follow the principles listed here:

· Furniture is well placed when it promotes conversation. Placing furniture in the middle of the space forces it to be used, and makes the room work better and feel bigger than when furniture is shoved to the perimeter of the room.
· Make sure the furniture highlights the room's best feature, rather than obstructs it.
· Take cues from the room itself. A chandelier, for instance, tells you where the table goes. If you need to move the table off centre, then swag the chain and install a second hook over the centre of the table so it casts light over dinner.
· Create comfortable conversation groupings no larger than 10 or 12 feet square. These areas should consist of a sofa or loveseat, coffee table and at least two chairs (or another loveseat). Arrange a grouping in front of the focal point. If there's no obvious focal point (fireplace, window, etc.), create one—a piano, music area, a sculpture, armoire or art.
· Position the largest pieces first, then gather the chairs around in a defined area with clear, unobstructed paths (about three feet wide) running past and not through the grouping. Make sure to leave 18 inches between sofa and coffee table. Chair and sofa seats should be about the same height. If the largest object in a room is on

one side, balance the other side of the room by placing more than one smaller object there.

· Anchor the grouping with a rug to give focus to the conversation area. Make sure to leave some breathing space in the arrangement. If furniture is squished on top of the carpet, either get a larger carpet, or move the furniture back off the rug, so the space looks bigger.

· If the sofa has its back to you on entry, position a sofa table behind and display a vase or small stack of books.

· If it's a large or long room, create secondary seating arrangements—vignettes or rooms within a room—to create a more human scale. For example, position a comfy chair or writing desk off by itself near the window.

· Gather seating around rather than across—it's more conversational, less interview style.

· Place low furniture in front of windows, because buyers gravitate to windows so they can look out; backless settees or lounges don't obstruct the view at all and visually expand space.

· Think proportion. Balance lower-slung furniture with a taller item such as a bookcase, wingback chair or even a display ladder against the wall.

· Contrast provides interest. Vertical items such as lamps, plant stands and entertainment units should balance horizontal pieces such as coffee table and sofa. Round pieces—sofa arms, round or oval mirrors, certain ottomans—can work

toward softening a room filled with too many angles. For example, with lean, tailored seating, add a round, tufted ottoman.

· Every home needs a dining space. If you have none, carve one out of your existing space—even a cloth draped on a small round table in a corner of the living room, accompanied by two upholstered chairs, indicates that you're ready for dinner. And it shows that your space can accommodate all the necessary functions.

Scale and proportion

Diane Chaput has been through hundreds of houses in her long career as an agent and she says that a home instantly telegraphs a sense of well-being—or not. She's found that when she brings this up with the homeowners, nine times out of ten they've already had the same feeling, but they just weren't sure why. She will leave them with a few brief suggestions, and return a week later to find the problem's been corrected.

The sense of well-being often comes from the proper relationship of scale and proportion. If the relationship between those two is off, then a sense of unease will reign. As Alexandra Stoddard writes in *The Decoration of Houses*, "It's immediately noticeable, a feeling that something's unstable—tiny end tables beside a massive sofa, or a few tall armoires in a low ceilinged room."

Since scale and proportion, along with principles such as balance and harmony, are the backbone of

Tomasz Majcherczyk

interior design, they're crucial to consider when rearranging your furniture and floor plan.

· **Scale** refers to similarity in dimension or size. Large-scale furniture (overstuffed couches, large armoires) *usually* works better in large rooms with high ceilings than in small rooms. That said, it's better to have a few well-chosen pieces of larger-scale furniture in a small room than several small delicate items, as long as the decorative details aren't exaggerated: for example, squared-off arms are all right, but extremely large rolled arms or Alice in Wonderland backs dwarf a smaller space. With fewer but larger pieces, the room has a well-organized, uncluttered look.

· Condo-sized furniture can often give you the scale you want but in a smaller footprint (footprint refers to the floor space it occupies) so that it physically fits into a small space. Sofas with low arms or none at all also work in a small space because they don't take up as much visual space.

· **Proportion** is the relation of one object to the whole space around it. In Heather's living room (seen below) two simple white loveseats and a slender coffee table are a trifle small for the room, but the three tall graphic artworks over the fireplace correct the imbalance and the grouping doesn't look lost.

· Proportion differs from scale in that it's determined by shape, form, line, curves and design details. A piece has either graceful or awkward proportions regardless of its scale—a wingback chair has intrinsically beautiful proportions, even though it might be out of scale with a cramped, low-ceilinged room.

· Proportion can feel not quite right if the scale of the dining table is out of whack with the chairs. Even the candlesticks must be proportionate to the centrepiece in order for it all to work.

· **Balance** is achieved through symmetry (mirror images on either side of a centre point) or asymmetry (non-identical items on either side of a centre point which carry the same visual weight). Symmetry is more common in traditional interiors, while asymmetry is generally found more in modern spaces, although both these rules have been broken successfully.

· **Harmony** refers to a unity of elements (material and colour palette) with enough variety to make it interesting. Harmony can be achieved through consistency—the repetition of shapes, colours, materials and textures. For a room to feel right, there must be a consistent theme—whether it's eclectic, country, transitional or traditional—

that's also carried throughout the home. That said, you can mix rustic country elements in a modern interior without creating disharmony, but there should be a similar mix throughout the house.

· **Negative/positive space**: Positive space is a filled area, while negative space is an unfilled area. Corridors and other circulation areas are usually negative space, while rooms with furniture are positive space. You can have too much positive space when you cram any room with too much, or things of the wrong scale for the room.

· A glass coffee table has more negative space than a solid table, because its form and density are less, which is also why it works well in a small room—there's visual breathing room.

· Most people are a little uneasy in an empty room, because there's too much negative space. That's why empty houses often sit on the market.

· When looking at your room layout, consider the *density*. Balance can be achieved by mixing

Tomasz Majcherczyk

pieces of different densities (for example, two leggy armchairs, a sofa with tailored skirt, and a round, tufted ottoman with no skirt).

Altering Your Inventory

Once you've examined each room and its space and architectural features, look at your inventory (furniture, accessories, lighting, etc.) and list what fits in each room. Take into consideration the scale, proportion, style, function, comfort and aesthetic appeal of each piece. Trot out your best-quality pieces—they will elevate the whole feel of your home.

Keep the following points in mind when altering your inventory:

· Don't be afraid to mix periods or finishes, as long as there's an integral link between the elements. In Heather's staging project, she placed whitewashed chairs around a wonderful old French table on castors. With a modern white chandelier, a beautiful white mirror and hurricane lamps with big white candles as a centrepiece, the mix is wonderfully French country. In Julia's house, new maple chairs on the Old Quebec theme with catgut seats were added to the antique pine harvest table. The various woods were of a similar enough tone and look (Canadiana) that they worked well together.

· Sometimes painting all the furniture one colour or tone works wonders with mismatched or tired-looking woods. An unexpected paint or stain on a piece of furniture can make you see it in a new light—my two mismatched porch chairs (one a wicker rocker, the other an unattractive 1940s number) are completely different chairs now that they're both painted black; they're stunning against the red brick. Refrain from painting, though, if the finish is in good shape, or if the piece will lose its value by doing so.

· Slipcovers in stretchy fabrics that fit snugly to the furniture are a great way of coordinating a room. (Quick tip for slipcovers: Velcro makes for a tight fit that looks upholstered.) But first determine if you'll want the piece in your new house; if you've never really liked it, then get rid of it and either rent or buy new.

· Sometimes only one element needs toning down—to test, tuck a cream-coloured canvas sheet around the offending item, and see how the others fare. You may only need to slipcover this one item (or store it off-site), then add cushions or throws to pick up the colours of the other furniture. Chaput says she has seen amazing things done with a throw—"all of a sudden that blue chair that had no business being there seems to fit right in."

· Buy plain white mattelasse covers from HomeSense (three or four doubles should do a sofa), pre-wash them to avoid shrinkage, and have the upholsterer make a slipcover for your sofa—very French, very chic and very cheap!

Tomasz Majcherczyk

Right: Mismatching furniture is fine as long as there's something unifying to tie the disparate elements together. In the case of this dining room, the table and chairs all have simplified details—rounded without being too ornate—while the art is simultaneously graphic and organic, and again without overdoing the embellishment. Tying it all together is the simple neutral colour scheme, punctuated with occasional bursts of colour, such as the small oriental runner beneath the table. The stager, Heather Shaw, found all the items in various locations—consignment shops, a high-end lighting store's discounted section, from her own and the real estate agent's homes.

· I inherited a double bed frame with nice details. Painted and propped against the wall, with tons of piled-high pillows, the headboard creates a much-needed focal point that makes the bedroom a glam retreat.

· Tone down formal rooms with furniture in low-maintenance, sturdy fabrics, and casual area rugs—today's lifestyles are much less formal. Bamboo place mats and a seagrass carpet totally changes the look of the ubiquitous mahogany Duncan Phyfe dining room set.

· Consider using furniture, rugs and accessories from other parts of your home. Look for items that will fit into your new arrangement and have colours or themes that harmonize with the room.

Where to get furniture for staging

Sometimes your home just doesn't have enough furniture—or enough of the right stuff. If you expect to buy new things for your next home, it might be worthwhile to purchase ahead of time and use those pieces for staging. In Heather's project, the homeowner had purchased a sectional for her new home, and found that it filled the family room of the other house perfectly.

If you have time to browse, check out flea markets, second-hand shops and estate sales—these places are great for finding coffee, end and sofa tables, and dining tables. Look for items that have clean, modern lines or that can be easily mixed with your own items.

Carry a scrapbook with your swatches, colours, and photos of existing furniture, and always have a measuring tape with you, and the measurements you're looking for. When buying second-hand upholstered goods, pick neutral colours—otherwise you'll want to reupholster, which can be fairly costly. The bottom line when buying for staging—whether new or used furniture—is make sure you really like it, because it's a substantial investment. If time is tight, or you're really not sure about what to buy, it's better to rent.

Nora Lukss says renting furniture makes sense because you can pick exactly what you need from vast resources of furniture, lighting, artwork and accessories. (See Resources for where to rent furniture.) However, it can also be very expensive, and Nora finds that sometimes all the home needs is one really fantastic piece, which homeowners can buy and take to their new place.

Stager Heather Shaw, on the other hand, frequently purchases things from a local consignment shop to fill a home. Spending as much as $5,000, she was able to bring the items back for resale as soon as the listing was sold. After all the consignment fees, Heather was only out of pocket $2,000—not bad for a whole house of furniture, especially considering the store had its own van for delivery and pick-up.

Last but not least, don't forget the kindness of strangers and friends. Raid friends' homes for things that will spruce up your interior, or do a temporary exchange—your cat-scratched club chair for their Ultrasuede ultra-chic dining chairs. (Just promise to have your cats vacate the premises for the duration.)

CHAPTER 6
COLOUR IT SOLD *The Challenge of Palettes*

Colour is probably the most difficult aspect of interior design to tackle, which is why most of us play it safe with taupe or beige, especially when listing a house for sale.

The instinct is right: light or pale colours keep space open and airy. But I've been in too many of these taupe and beige homes—and probably you have too—to believe that this safe colour choice is successful in making people want to linger.

I decided to seek the advice of my friend Shelley Kirsch, an extremely busy residential designer who is probably the best colourist I know. I've been in many a project of hers, each one different from the next, but all abounding in comfort and beauty. You immediately want to come in, plop down and never leave—which is exactly what you want your buyer to do.

Part of the equation for a feel-good interior (as described in the previous chapter) is proper scale, proportion, balance and flow. Another major component is colour. While Kirsch is a big fan of colour, she also says it can never compete with the house and its flow. "It's no mystery that everyone wants space—nobody wants to move into a closet. Creating space is your starting point and everything you do is trying to highlight that simple fact."

Easier said than done, perhaps. For one thing, she says, pure, natural colours do not translate well into an interior. "Trying to copy nature exactly is a trap—the verdant green you find in nature looks awful inside. People want to make their home feel like the seashore, or the cottage, because that makes them feel relaxed. That's a good thing. But you can't bring that blue of the water into your home, and expect it to translate into a water feel. There are too many issues with light—incandescent, as well as the reflection from outdoors."

That said, in the house featured in this chapter, relating to the outdoors was important. It backed onto a gorgeous ravine that was previously unseen from the interior because the kitchen window was tiny. Once Kirsch reconfigured the interior space, evened out the staggered ceiling heights and added windows, the spectacular view became apparent—and it set the tone for the rest of the main floor.

When Kirsch created a colour palette, she opted for interpretations of nature in much the same way that an artist interprets landscapes in her paintings.

What colours to use, and where to start?

Kirsch says you must start from the home's context and existing vernacular—the architecture, the setting, the windows, lights, upholstery and floor colour.

In the house Kirsch worked on, the ravine dictated a natural palette of linen, pale mustard, sun-dried tomato, celery, plus a few more vibrant colours (like dill pickle and eggplant) for blocking and punctuation. The house has a lot of natural materials—natural oak and cherry, natural stone counters—which were "sympathetic" to the ravine setting, but had to be considered in the interior palette as well.

The general geography of the area is also important to consider. Kirsch says, "Cobalt and white and fuchsia may work really well in Australia, but not here in Toronto where clouds and deciduous trees figure largely. The palette has to balance the area in an anchored way." High-energy colours work in a sunny locale, but they

can also work in a dark basement that needs an infusion of warm energy.

In designer Alexandra Stoddard's view, the colour should make a home feel happy. "Muddy colours are not happy," she writes in *The Decoration of Houses*. "Many people prefer dirt-camouflaging colours because they're safer, but it does affect your mood…if you can have clear colours, why choose something cloudy? Just by being inside you're deprived of sunlight; you need clear fresh colours and lots of white to counteract the particular darkness cast by walls that diminish the energy from light." Stoddard says that organic materials such as wood (in butcher block counters), marble (on tables and floors) and cork (for flooring) are energizing, but that "bland artificial neutral tones are more likely to shut down, not soothe, the human spirit."

Stoddard's advice is simple: "Never live with a colour that dampens your spirit; there's a reason cheerful, inspiring people live with fresh colours, they recognize instinctively the powerful emotional feelings colours evoke; what interior spaces cry out for is clear tints of colour."

That's not to say that yellow is the obvious choice. In fact, Kirsch says many people make the mistake of thinking yellow will create sunshine in a dark house. "It's the hardest colour to get right. And in a traditional house with natural wood trim, the combination of brown and yellow is just not an appealing juxtaposition." A much better

Andrew Filarski

colour choice for natural wood, she believes, is blue grey, or grey-green, and even red, strong blue, or celery.

When done properly, colour can stir the senses of even the most hardened buyer.

The reality of staging, though, is that when you need to do it, it's usually too late to dally over paint chips for any length of time. And you may not have the time to repaint the whole house in this wonderful new scheme. In that situation, Kirsch suggests developing a scheme that "complements the sofa or drapery fabric, tiles in the kitchen, broadloom on the floors." She advises: "Don't paint every room a completely different colour, as it is distracting. Know who your house is going to appeal to. If you have a first-time-buyer type of house, you can safely assume that starting a family might be under consideration. If you have three bedrooms, paint two of them in similar tones and perhaps paint the third in a tone that might say 'appropriate for nursery.' If you have a 'move-up' house, keep things neutral with some colour work in the vestibule, powder room and dining room."

What about the idea of coordinating the whole house with one colour for better flow?

There are some good examples and some bad examples of this. When Kirsch first saw the house featured in these photos, it was painted dusty rose—colour coordinated for sure, but very dated and the pink was too strong a presence to cover every wall.

Besides, coordination doesn't always mean one colour. She suggests, instead, taking your favourite paint company's fandeck (the full complement of colour swatches, usually available in a stack that fans out for viewing and comparing paint

Right: Rather than simply contrast dark and light, Kirsch has made subtle transitions from dark to light, by introducing medium tones. Pale celery walls continue into the dining room area, for example, and are punctuated by pimento dining chairs; the red is a middle tone that segues into the dark wood of the handsome dining table, the deep eggplant wall near the back door, and the dark brown wall-mounted console cabinet.

Shelley Kirsch's quick tips include: light wood floors reflect light, and dark wood floors draw colour down; painting crown moulding the same colour as the ceiling will make the room feel taller and draw your eye up; built-ins versus free-standing pieces will expand your space; painting wood furniture the same colour as the walls makes a room look bigger.

Look at colours in different lighting: inside with the lights on, with lights off, when the sun goes down, and in the brightest part of the morning. There's a big fluctuation of colour, and it's amazing how chameleon-like some colours are.

Check the chip vertically against the wall, rather than in the palm of your hand, then test it against other objects in the room.

chips), and choosing a colour family—greens, yellows, blues, tans, white/cream/sand. Then you can choose colours in that fan, one or two tones up or down, giving you a whole house scheme. (But remember that paint on the walls is much more intense than on the chip—see below for tips.)

A continuous colour, depending on the colour of course, creates better flow in the house because it causes visual space to expand since there's more space for the eye to wander. This applies even when adjoining rooms are painted different tones of the same colour (a monochromatic scheme), and includes baseboards, moulding and doors.

As long as colours complement one another, you should be able to get away with not painting, especially if there's not the time or budget for it, as long as the paint still looks fresh. In Julia's staging project, the living and dining rooms were yellow and green, and when the furniture was flipped for better layout, it also made more sense colour-wise. If your living room has pale blue walls, chocolate furnishings and ivory drapes, and the dining room has blue chair seats, think about chocolate walls and blue and ivory patterned damask drapes (bought off the rack from a big box store), and displaying only creamware in the china cabinet.

Your chosen colour scheme can be carried upstairs to the bedrooms, though many designers prefer big colour in the main floor gathering spaces, with a more restrained palette in the retreat areas— bedrooms, spa baths and second-floor family rooms, for instance. Just make sure that the transition from main floor to second isn't too jarring—for example, a creamy yellow, celery and ivory scheme on the main floor shouldn't lead you to a cherry-red teen's room, an orange little girl's room. Paint them in something more complementary, such as blues, sage green or even lime.

If you're starting from scratch and can do the whole house, pick four or five tones in a row on the fandeck, and work with a variation on this theme. On that basis, Kirsch suggests keeping the ceilings

in the palest tone, the walls in the mid-tone. If the baseboards are nothing to write home about, paint them out in the same colour as the walls, then move up two more tones for accents such as a colour-blocked wall and the door. Or, as in the vestibule of this house, create horizontal stripes with two tones of the same colour. This will keep the environment fluid.

You could also take a graduated-tone approach—that is, the living room in one tone, the dining room two tones up, and the entry two tones down. It can be very successful, when there are good natural barriers, such as archways, that mark the shift.

What about using colour as a punctuation point, as in colour blocking?

This can be tricky, Kirsch says—basically, you have to know when to provoke and when to keep quiet. But if you're selling your house and want to add some colour without repainting everything, colour blocking can be a time-saver, and very effective. For example, in the bedroom, take into consideration the sheets and carpet, and paint the headboard wall in a complementary colour for a little punch. Choose a tone from something that already exists in the room. This will give a little drama without making the room seem to close in.

In the bath, you can use colourful towels to highlight a very pale colour scheme. It doesn't have to be cobalt blue and lime green, it can be salmon jacquard in a light brown room, or seafoam green and white in a pale blue room.

A terrific piece of art over the sofa or on the mantel, is a good opportunity for colour blocking.

Kirsch colour-blocked some areas—like the chocolate-eggplant colour on the small wall behind the breakfront in the dining area. And the one dill pickle wall in the family bathroom provides a lively and startling contrast to the otherwise quiet black and white scheme.

Are there areas where you can take risks?

It depends on how you look at risks. A white living room, looking into a white dining room, is a little deathly, Kirsch finds, so pumping some colour into that isn't taking a risk, but doing necessary resuscitation.

White is a definite choice—and not an avoidance of colour—though an all-white scheme can be a challenge to pull off. In bright rooms, the right white glows. In dark rooms, like basements, white can read grey especially in the shadows.

Effectively using white can be done by layering creams, ivories and sand colours that will give you a rippling effect with movement, refinement and a certain purity of light and style. An all-white room can look great—pure, clean and fresh. But it can also be monotonous unless you add texture, such as shag or Berber carpeting, damask bed linens, thick towels, cashmere throws, natural wood floors, some wood furniture and houseplants.

There are areas where Kirsch likes to crank up the colour: the dining room, the powder room and the front entry.

The dining room has always been associated with celebrating, so she believes it can stand a jolt of colour that you might avoid in other rooms: red chairs around a modern table, an eggplant wall backing a low-slung breakfront, decorative overhead pendant lighting, and pale celery bamboo window shades.

Okay, but aren't there times that colour needs to be quiet?

"The broadest strokes—walls, ceiling and large furnishings—should be non-competitive and in a similar colour family, which allows you to punctuate with accents," Kirsch says.

The largest piece of furniture should be very close to the wall colour—so if you're casting about for a wall colour, take inspiration from the sofa. "That choice will also give a sense of openness because when walls and upholstery are tonally connected, you have a chance to breathe." On the other hand, she says, "If you have a navy blue sofa, don't paint the whole room navy, but look for a tonally connected colour. Then choose an element to echo it elsewhere—a navy-framed mirror or piece of art—so that the navy-blue isn't sticking out like a beacon."

You want a room with a lot of seating to feel as open as possible, she continues. Keep the largest pieces uncluttered (that is, no skirts, swags or huge piles of cushions). And if you're renting furniture in order to sell the house, pick out neutrals and add colour through accessories—pillows, rugs and art objects. Drapery, too, is part of the equation, and needs to feel tonally connected to the walls, rather than work as punctuation, Kirsch says. "Otherwise there's a shrinkage of space, where the two tones and colours meet, and you don't want people to feel that way."

How Colour Works

Colour is reflected light, so natural light affects how it looks. For example, blue can turn to purple at sunset, coral in the morning can look yellow in the afternoon and orange at night. Pale blue or grey is fresh and crisp in south-facing areas, but facing north it can be cold. Where natural light is low, a warm neutral shade reflects light and is more comfortable and inviting.

Colour is generally described by hue (what colour it is) saturation (how pure or strong it is) and lightness (how much white or black the hue contains). Colours are classified as warm (reds, yellows and oranges), cool (blues, greens and purples) or neutral (beiges, browns, blacks, greys and whites). Light colours feel spacious; dark ones are cozy; bright ones can energize.

Weight refers to the depth of a colour. The deeper a colour, the weightier (or heavier) it is. Muddy colours that are soft in daylight can be heavy at night; warm colours that are cozy by night can be overpowering in the daylight. For staging—and for living—mid-tones read light and soft during the day, and luminous at night—which is what you want when you're selling.

Rooms used primarily at night can take stronger colours; rooms used during the day are better in paler colours. (But light also has a huge effect on this, too.) Considering that buyers may be touring your house at any time of the day or evening, it's safer to stick with pale, warm colours. But also

COLOUR TERMS

Neutral: little or no colour saturation (white, grey, black)

Warm: yellow, orange and red. These advance, making the wall or object look closer.

Cool: blue, green and purple/lavender. These recede, making the wall or object appear farther.

Pastel: light, saturated colours with a lot of white base

Value: a colour's lightness or darkness

Tone: a colour's greyness—how much black has been added

Heavy: dark colours in the cool range which are not very saturated

Deep: dark, saturated colours

Open: light, unobtrusive colours

Left: The same colour scheme continues on the main floor into the home office-den.

is what will stand out. A white with a warm undertone has more yellow, red or orange in the tinting. A cool white has more blue or green. In a poorly lit room, such as a basement, white can look grey and dingy, so a better choice would be a warmer tone that can replace natural light. So, pick the white you like, then go one to two shades lighter. If you can't find the exact lighter chip, then ask for the paint to be mixed one-half or three-quarters of the full formula.

Beiges and off-whites do have subtle colouration, so compare paint chips to your fabrics and flooring to determine if a warmer, pink- or yellow-toned white, versus a cooler, blue-toned white is best for your room.

Taupey off-whites are soothing, but you have to be careful that they don't read as pink once they're on the walls. When choosing any white, hold it against a colour chip that has the same tones. If, for example, that taupey off-white reads pink against a solid taupe chip, then you know it will probably show up on the wall. When choosing white, start by eliminating all the undertones you don't like (and you'll be able to tell by doing the solid colour chip test described above).

Primary colours

Yellow, this mimic of sunshine, is usually a cheerful, warm, happy colour. It works well in large quantities as long as the tone is not too strong. Creamy butter tones work well in living

remember that some colours when made pale look pastel—not a good thing.

Colour affects moods—cherry red, chocolate brown and Mediterranean orange are all drama, while charcoal, mauve and silver are sensuous, and blush pink or tranquil blue are sweet. When staging, you don't want buyers either shocked or tranquilized, but soothed, happy, comfortable and welcomed.

Colour changes depending on what objects are around it. A red sofa will melt into a red wall, but against a caramel wall it pops out. A blue chair next to a white wall will give the wall a blue-green cast, so yellow or tan on the wall works better.

White

There's no such thing as pure white, so when selecting a white paint look at the undertones, because once the paint dries, that undertone rooms, halls and nurseries; mid-tones are fine in bedrooms and kitchens. It's a good hue for entries where there are no windows, but strong yellows are too aggressive, especially for staging.

Blue is another primary. Cool and receding, it's the colour of water and sky—relaxing, meditative and refreshing. Mixed with white it's crisp; add yellow and you have a Provence summer.

Red is the colour of energy, warmth, passion and excitement. Because it's a colour that demands attention, whenever you put something red in a room that object will take precedence over others. Red is wonderful in small doses but can easily overwhelm. For staging, red is better left out of your wall palette, though you might consider using it for impact in a dining room.

Secondary colours

Secondary colours come from mixing equal parts of two primary colours. Red and yellow create orange; red and blue make purple; and green is a mixture of yellow and blue. Green is the most common secondary colour to use in an interior—it's the soothing colour of nature and is good to have in some amount in every space. Again, though, keep in mind that you should keep greens toned down, rather than trying to imitate nature exactly.

Pattern and texture

No discussion of colour is complete without introducing the idea of pattern and texture—the fabrics and finishes that will be chosen to go with a particular colour.

Because a contemporary interior has very little pattern and very minimal coloration, it relies on texture for visual interest—for example, nubbly chenille on sofas and chairs, silk pillows and drapes, art objects in iron or other metals, handwoven throws, blown-glass vases, sleek modern pottery and natural stone floors.

Pattern is to be expected in a traditional interior, but you don't need much—a plaid mohair throw, a striated glass vase, a tapestry chair, vertical stripe curtains to exaggerate window height.

Whatever your style, pare back on shiny fabrics for staging—you may love your shiny satins and embossed furniture, but they can look too formal for staging. They can be offset with a casual all white throw, or pillows in natural fibres. If you really want a little sparkle, better to bring it in with a mirror or two, and the odd accessories in pewter or silver.

Pattern can also be introduced by way of flooring. Tiles laid on the bias add a diamond pattern, and effectively widen a long, narrow room. Painting wide stripes of the same coloured paint, but alternating matte and semi-gloss, gives the barest suggestion of pattern and texture on walls.

Wallpaper usually provides pattern and texture, but has to be handled carefully, especially when staging. Wallpaper can quickly become dated, so if it's not a classic—stripes, toile or grasscloth, for example—remove it if possible. But please don't paint over it—seams showing beneath the paint just look sloppy.

Quick tips for pulling it all together

· A sample board with swatches, paint chips and material samples gives you an idea of how it will all look together; try it out in every area to see how light and shade affect the colours.

· Colour trends change. A teal blue wall is so 1980s buyers will run screaming. If you really love the colour, then buy a glass vase in it, but leave the walls sand, and you've created a soothing water theme.

· Colour always looks darker on the wall than on the chip, so go two shades lighter when buying.

· Paint looks different wet than dry, so don't despair—like I did—when your lovely green looks like pea soup. Wait a day, then weep if it's still the same hideous shade.

· For less than $10, you can try out that "perfect" colour with a pint or litre to cover part of a wall (or, better yet, a piece of board for ease of movement from room to room).

· For $25 you can get Home Hardware's software program called HomeWorks to see exactly what your room will look like in a different colour.

· Finishes: use flat or eggshell on walls, flat on ceilings, and semi-gloss on woodwork, trim and cabinets.

· If ceilings are low, go with pale walls and dark floors—it will give the illusion of higher ceilings.

· Dark, warm colours will make a large room feel cozier.

· Strong natural light in a room heats up warm colours, so lean toward paler, cooler colours in this situation.

· In a room with little light, stick with warm but pale to add light and energy.

· A long and narrow hall will be foreshortened with a dark end wall. Conversely, unattractive trim, vents, rads or an ugly fire door will recede when painted the same colour as the walls.

· No time to paint over a loud wall? Minimize the colour by placing more furniture against it, or by applying a wash or glaze to tone down the colour (ask at your paint store how to do this).

· Use large paint cards or create your own test swatches whenever possible. Many paint companies now provide test-size containers, and some offer paint cards as large as 12-inches by 12-inches.

Tomasz Majcherczyk

CHAPTER 7

LIGHT *The Biggest Bang for Your Buck*

Nothing sells a home like light, especially in northern climates such as ours. Light enhances a feeling of well-being, and makes even small spaces seem larger. Light is such a precious commodity that stagers say not having enough is one of the biggest drawbacks of trying to sell a home.

This is particularly true of older homes. Designed to retain heat within four walls, the rooms of an older house can be dark and close, with few windows. Modern insulation has more or less solved the heat retention problem, so there's less need for interior walls, and windows can be larger. New and renovated homes reflect these differences. But if light still eludes you in your unrenovated Victorian, don't despair—there are ways to bring it in.

Natural light

The best way to brighten your home is to bring in more natural light. Although it's a large undertaking, removing one or more interior walls, either fully or partially, could be your best bet. It's usually very messy, requiring the removal of old plaster and lath, and you'll almost certainly have to patch the floor where the wall was, since it's likely that the finished flooring is only built up to the sides of the wall rather than running underneath it. Keep in mind that you'll have to check out the structural feasibility with a registered designer or architect, and will need a building permit as well. Still, if taking out the wall brings in a great deal more light, or radically improves the flow of the space, investing the time and money could yield a substantial return when you sell.

But bringing in natural light can also be as simple as replacing heavy drapes with filmy, gauzy sheers. Or switching rooms around to take advantage of light at the time of day when the room is being used—like a dark living room and a light-filled formal dining room. Or taking the interior doors off the doorways to your living room and/or dining room. French doors in place of solid

Stager Gerine de Jong

wood allow light to flow through, and they're less than $200 unpainted. And if you happen to be replacing the windows, go bigger, and enlarge the opening. Consider this only if the house is a really dark and poky pit, because you'll need to rebuild the frame; this will be pricey and will also alter the look of the exterior. Skylights, on the other hand, are great light creators and can be installed fairly inexpensively—just make sure you get a professional to do it.

Artificial light

No matter how much natural light your home has, you still need to supplement with artificial light. This comes in three forms: general (overall lighting), task (focused lighting) and accent (highlight and sparkle-effect lighting).

Because general lighting is usually overhead—as in a central fixture or recessed lights—it can be less

than flattering for the inhabitants, creating shadows right where you don't want them (under the eyes). Task lighting can balance these patterns of light, and redirect shadows. As its name implies, this kind of lighting helps you perform tasks—such as reading, preparing dinner or working in a home office. Accent lighting adds drama and visual interest by spotlighting individual items, such as a painting, plant or sculpture. Its intensity needs to be about three times that of the general light around it for the object to stand out.

A lighting scheme should have a mix of brightness and wattage through a variety of light sources. In rooms you're happy to highlight, use higher-wattage bulbs, but if you want to create mood or minimize flaws, cut back on the wattage and invest in dimmers for every light so you can moderate the levels.

Different light sources have different characteristics. Incandescent, for example, gives off warm light, halogen is cooler, brighter and whiter, while traditional fluorescent can be greenish, and has a tendency to hum (the new low-energy fluorescents don't, however). Amber filament bulbs, now readily available, give a candle-like glow, especially flattering in the hallway, living room or bedroom.

Lighting is cheap if you head to a building supply store or discount home store. In very high-end homes it might be better to buy from a specialty shop.

In the kitchen

The more illumination choices in this room, the better. Either extend existing track lighting or install new, and point the light source at the front of pantry cabinets, wall ovens and on the counters for great effect.

Under-cabinet fixtures shed additional light on counters. Simple plug-in halogen lights give bright, clear light, and can be attached to a dimmer. Inexpensive disposable strip lighting is another way to bring in light, and is easily installed with two-faced tape. When bulbs burn out you simply replace the entire unit.

If your kitchen is part of an open concept area, put the task lights on dimmers so you can raise or lower the light depending on the mood you're after.

In the living room

Table and floor lamps with incandescent bulbs offer the most comfortable, flattering lighting. Add a gold-lined shade for an even warmer glow, or silver-lined for a bit of sparkle. Most shades that go with lamps are too big, so consider buying smaller ones separately—readily available at stores like HomeSense. The lampshades in any given room need to be of a similar scale and look to reduce visual clutter.

Reinvent your garage sale or flea market lamp with a beautiful new shade. You can find these just about anywhere, or you can create your own with beaded or tasselled trim (available from any fabric store) added to the outside or inside of the shade. If a lamp is small, elevate it on a bookshelf, a stack of books, a highboy chest or mantel. You can also place small lamps or spot lights behind plants or on top of armoires to add variety and balance to the lighting scheme and to accent a specific area.

In rooms where there is only one window, place the light source on the opposite side of the room. Be generous with table lamps—anything between three and five is fine for most rooms. That includes wall sconces which create a three-dimensional element to your lighting scheme—add paper or glass shades for a diffuse glow.

Use dimmer switches on both overhead and task lights to cut down on harsh, bright light when the mood or time of day changes.

In the bedroom

Light both sides of the bed with lamps on night tables if there's room, but if there's no floor space at least add wall-mounted reading lamps on either side of the bed. Chandeliers are fun and romantic in the bedroom, and add sparkle with low-level wattage. Take the chandelier from the dining room and replace that one with something more modern.

In the dining room

If the dining table is long, hang two or more pendant lights over the table to emphasize its length and make a grand statement. It's also a more modern look. Think outside the box—the chandelier doesn't have to be brass. Antique stores have lots of nickel, silver, pewter and chrome-plate beauties to choose from. You could also purchase an inexpensive chandelier and paint it either white or matte black.

For a sparkly effect, light your glass or china collection from inside glass-front cupboards or the breakfront.

In hallways, stairs and landings
Good illumination is important in these areas, but it shouldn't overpower. For a bit of drama, install pendant lights, especially the large hurricane type with glass.

Tricks to create light
Dark walls suck up the light. Period. If your walls are deep and saturated, give serious consideration to repainting. One way to create sunshine is through paint—pale, creamy yellows, or smooth pumpkin evokes the sunny Mediterranean life. Even pale robin's egg blue gives a crisp lift to any interior.

Mirrors can be used to great advantage—a large mirror in the darker middle rooms of the house will reflect light. It also reflects a view and expands the visual horizons. Other reflective surfaces, like glass-topped and wrought iron coffee tables, bounce light and add sparkle. In a narrow hallway, mirrors hung on the walls will effectively double the width, but stick with a few large ones, rather than several smaller pieces, to avoid the house of mirrors effect. In small rooms, place mirrors next to the window as long as the bounced view is an attractive one.

There's a low overhanging porch blocking sunlight into our living room—once the dark cedar ceiling was painted a bright white, the difference inside was immediately noticeable.

Windows
Window treatments are an important finishing touch in any room. But if you're changing them or adding to stage your home, keep it simple for cost and time reasons. You can get ready-made Roman shades, blinds and drapery panels just about anywhere and they're inexpensive. On the other hand, Jennifer Brouwer swears by the effect of custom-made drapery on potential buyers—many people love to know that's taken care of, she says.

Rods and panels tend to be a more traditional approach, but can complement a modern interior if the fabric's right. Just make sure to hang them high, as near the ceiling as possible, to draw the eye up and increase the sense of height. Install rods wide of the window frame to maximize light. It's best to put up rods before measuring for fabric—otherwise you may end up with drapes not reaching the floor.

In traditional French homes, two sets of drapes usually fill the window, an inner sheer or translucent silk for a shimmery glow, and a heavier outer layer in velvet or brocade. While this evokes a certain lush look, it might be a bit much if the furnishings don't reflect the theme you're going for. If you do hang only panels on either side of the window, make sure they're either backed by a heavier fabric lining, or that the fabric is full enough to look like a drape—otherwise, they can look like two limp sticks on either side of the window.

Swing-arm rods allow curtains in tight spaces, such as when a window is close to a wall, and gives the finished look of drapes without obstructing light. A window valance over sliding glass doors hides the metal track. For a temporary treatment, try tension rods inside a window frame draped with a sheer or fabric.

If you want to minimize an awful view—like the neighbour's brick wall or an unsightly fire escape—try matchstick blinds, opaque roller blinds, magnetic roller shades, gauzy Roman shades, or plantation shutters. Where windows are small, especially in basements, hang drapes high and wide (or use plantation shutters) to give the illusion of big windows and suggest that there's "something else" behind there.

Window treatments should harmonize with the other elements of your room in either a complementary or contrasting way. Acid-green velvet drapes might sound like a strange choice in a contemporary home, but next to a white leather Mies lounger and an Eileen Grey side table, they'd be just the thing.

Another way to inject a room with "artificial" light is to have window treatments in the same pale colour as the wall—this creates a wall of lightness and doesn't impose on the room. As well, the light fabric won't suck up any extra light.

There's nothing to say you can't leave windows bare, especially if the view is terrific and the windows are an architectural feature in and of themselves. Of course, in every situation, the windowpanes must be sparkling clean.

Tomasz Majcherczyk

CHAPTER 8
ACCESSORIES *The Jewel in Your Real Estate Crown*

The jury's still out on how much to depersonalize your home when it's time to sell. Some stagers will tell you to take it all away, while others say you should keep at least some of it in. Real estate agent Diane Chaput says that she almost dreads when someone who is listing with her calls to say they've done the purge. "Inevitably they've gone too far, and there's nothing left of them in the house. Each home has a personality, and when you depersonalize, the house feels it." It's not uncommon to find Chaput before an agents' open house, snooping for accessories that are hiding so she can inject some life back into the house.

One practical disadvantage to paring back too much is that everything gets noticed in a room with little detail—fingerprints on a fridge, a stray hair on the bathroom floor, a crack in the wall.

Accessories are the jewels of interior décor, and in staging, they can be as important as furniture. A nice living room becomes exotic with a patchwork silk pillow. A tired bathroom becomes spa-like with a thick terrycloth shower curtain, beautiful towels and mats, heated towel racks, candles, bath tray and aromatherapy soaps. Accessories don't need to be expensive—a tassel on a cabinet door, a bowl of lemons, thick towels in a basket. They make an empty home feel lived in.

But accessories can also be expensive to rent or buy, says designer Jennifer Brouwer. That's when she starts raiding Grandma's attic, the best friend's basement, the local thrift store and the library's book sale cart.

Although I'm in favour of personal touches, accessories fall under the same rule of moderation as anything else. We usually have too much stuff, and our homes require some judicious editing and paring back. So rather than dozens of Red Rose tea miniatures lined up on a windowsill, pick three and place them in a small and unexpected nook.

Right: Four simple coat hooks under the window and five small cranberry glass vases on the sill create a "picture" out of this window.

Bottom right: When displaying accessories—in ones, threes or fives as a rule—make sure there's some consistency between elements, such as the tin or pewter metal of these objects, and mix up the heights.

Tomasz Majcherczyk

General display rules

Experiment and document your efforts with a digital camera to see how the display improves.

It's always better when your eye can step up and down from item to item. Loosely position items in overlapping triangles to create a sense of movement and layer: for example, a tall lamp, a stack of books and a tiny bud vase.

Blend practical and pretty. Make displays vertical and horizontal. Don't make your displays too generic—group according to style or colour. It's also about juxtaposition—what objects are next to one another, and how the objects influence each other. Think back to the child's game of determining what doesn't fit in this picture, and eliminate the one that stands out.

Display doesn't have to be elaborate—a pretty plate with seashells on the entry console, unfussy pottery dishes at the dining table, a pitcher filled with field flowers. Inside the front door, install four beautiful pewter coat hooks, but hang just one coat instead of 20.

Storage containers need to match, especially in the kitchen and bath: a row of glass candy jars on a shelf; cream porcelain for cotton swabs, cotton balls and tissues; portmeirion canisters. Straw baskets lined on shelves keep books, papers and toys tidily out of sight. Containers don't need to

be the ubiquitous wicker, though—a window box installed inside the window of a child's room can hold books and Lego, for instance.

Leave breathing room between objects. The space between objects should be less than the width of the stand-alone item. As a rule, odd numbers create more visual interest than even. The exception is modern interiors in which a gallery setting of six slim horizontally framed

Tomasz Majcherczyk

Tomasz Majcherczyk

pictures, or two tall prints side by side, can look stunning.

Keep style in mind when arranging accessories. A formal traditional room may call for luxurious velvet, tapestry and glittery finishes; a modern room needs almost no pattern, relying instead on tones and textures.

Start small when creating vignettes, keeping in mind that variety in height, weight, density,

Tomasz Majcherczyk

shape and textures is a good thing. For example, fill a hammered tin vase with silky orchids, or pair a glass candlestick next to a rough-hewn pot. Remember, too, that pieces need to have some connection, whether through their materials or colours. So a variety of containers, contrasted by height, should have similar colour or material: tall, hammered tin vase, short pewter bud vase, wide tin container and one pewter candle.

A bronze horse figure on its own might look lost, but add some well-worn antique leather-bound books and a small silver candlestick and you've created a scenario.

Cluster like objects together—glass vases on a windowsill, candles in the centre of a dining table, books stacked vertically and horizontally on a bookshelf but with lots of space to breathe around them. Instead of tiny things dotted all over the interior landscape, mass them together for more effect, or use just one large accessory.

It doesn't matter what items cost, as long as they complement each other. Luxury can be created by pairing a sumptuous large item with something smaller, as long as the one doesn't dwarf the other, and the contrast creates a sense of space.

People respond to touch, notes Paco Underhill, researcher of human shopping habits. He's found that people want to touch something the minute they enter a room, especially when a room has a good feeling. Burnished wood, down seating, thick pile rugs, handmade objects and solid brass door

Below: A simple table arrangement—two glass jars and a terracotta planter—telegraph the casual, but interesting nature of this home. The hutch shows a pared back collection of depression glass and blue willow.

handles are examples of things that people can run their hands along and will desire to touch. Walk through your home and let your hand tell you if your rooms are sufficiently tactile—you might respond to Ultrasuede furniture, thick towels, cool cotton bedding or a feather duvet. If there's nothing, add to the mix with items such as faux fur pillows, cashmere throws, rocks in a bowl or soft flannel upholstery.

Similarly, what do you *not* like to touch? Since buyers will likely be in their stocking feet, pull up scratchy rugs made of sisal or coir, and put down thick wool instead. (Cotton rugs with a generous underpad will accomplish the same.)

Take a look at things tucked away—is there a new spot for them? Julia discovered all sorts of accessories hidden away in a house she staged. The big pot on top of the living room armoire was in the crawlspace. A framed floral hiding behind a curtain in the bathroom now hangs on the wall of the guest room/home office. The antique steamship primitive—in a bookcase behind the living room door—now has pride of place on the black dresser in the master bedroom. In the upstairs hall, a glass-front bookcase was neatly filled with books and placed under a woodland print. Julia found two primitive folk art seagulls in a drawer and added her own small iron pot with dried flowers.

Tomasz Majcherczyk

As you can see from this house, the guideline for personalizing is simple: if it's beautiful, the appeal will be universal.

In a small space, large accessories work best—an oversized painting (or photocopy of painting, framed); antique mirrors or old picture frames refurbished with mirror glass, big wooden birdcages, large iron sconces or iron grate (like the one Julia placed over the master bed).

The general rule is to put away everything that's under 10-inches tall in order to create impact, but Julia's display often uses a few small pieces, and she has a good eye for what goes where, and how to juxtapose against larger pieces.

Architectural components make great accessories—but just one, please.

Glossy, healthy plants make a room feel alive and bring the outdoors in, but dying plants make a room look sick, so toss those out. Position one great plant for effect, or group several small plants en masse. Potted plants rather than fresh-cut flowers are cheaper and longer lasting. And in a house with low levels of light, think artificial—they make very real-looking ones these days.

Marco Pasanella, writing in *Living in Style Without Losing Your Mind*, lists a few things under $20 that every home should have: photographs, which make huge impact; goldfish, which are cheap,

Tomasz Majcherczyk

cheery and easy to care for (they are apparently the most soothing sleeping companions for humans); living herbs, which smell good and clean the air; lemons, which are less expensive than flowers; and big puffy towels.

Antique accessories soften a room's look. Think of Depression glass displayed in groupings on a buffet, old books stacked horizontally on a mantel, beat-up silver candlesticks on leather-bound books with gold-rimmed glasses beside, or a glass pitcher for fresh flowers.

Instead of a painting or photo over a bed, be creative—Julia placed a small wrought iron grate with dried coral-tipped baby roses over the bed. In the guest room, she brought her own white-washed metal basket filled with dried roses to hang over the bed, now draped with a metre of exquisite Pierre Frey fabric.

For more display ideas, check out online stores. Ralph Lauren Home and Laura Ashley (see Resources at back of book), for example, are great at display.

Quick tips:

· Identical picture frames give a clean, uninterrupted sightline through the room.
· Make art out of botanical prints, pressed flowers and leaves, or colour copies of an actual flower, in IKEA frames. You can also make great art out of photocopies of a black-and-white print (if you do colour copies, it comes out sepia toned).
· Buy a book of architectural prints, cut out the artwork and frame: hang three or five together for a gallery look.
· If you have a large wall, place one prominent piece of art on it, rather than several smaller items. Save the smaller pieces for a gallery row in a stairway or upstairs hall. If a wall is less than 30-inches it doesn't need any art.
· Display art at a focal point, or group it to make a focal point.
· Frame small pieces in very large mats and frames, which lend them an air of importance.
· Hang art on a wall of a contrasting colour.
· An accent colour used behind art will make it stand out.
· Hang artwork in proportion to the expanse of the wall. Avoid scattering or hanging small prints on large walls. Add textured items to your art groupings for added interest.
· Sculpture is a great addition to any room, adding height and a touch of the unexpected. Don't be afraid to mix periods, as long as they have a connecting thread; create a collage by grouping many small artworks together, linking them through visual forms, theme or colour. The pieces will play off one another to create a single graphic effect.

Room by room
Kitchen

· Herbs on windowsills look good and smell fresh.

- Straw baskets, pretty pottery cups and bowls can be displayed in glass-front cupboards.
- Display colourful china on open shelves.
- A bowl of limes or lemons on the counter, with a country pot filled with herbs, and two Perrier bottles makes a great natural arrangement; a big ceramic bowl of fresh fruit says welcome.
- Colourful small appliances—electric-blue toasters, fire-engine-red mixers, tangerine coffee makers—add interest and colour, but while your house is listed, limit these beauties to one and put the rest away.
- Add to the counter space and storage with a butcher block wire cart to hold appliances you use infrequently.
- For a relatively inexpensive new kitchen floor, look at Mexican clay tiles. Thick and chunky, they're forgiving of uneven subfloors, and when turned over have a pale and pretty underside, almost like limestone. If installed upside down, make sure to seal with polyurethane.

Dining room
- For a little shimmery luxury, paint the brass chandelier a pewter or nickel finish or a completely different colour—brown, bright blue, red. Car spray paint is the best product to use on metal because it adheres well.
- China displayed in a dining room breakfront can read as very formal, which is fine if the house you're listing is big and formal and can accommodate a separate dining room. But if the room also serves as the main eating area for the family, try toning down the look by displaying art, books and quirky items. I hot-glued pistachio-green fabric to the back of my breakfront, so it's a nice foil for white dishes and objects. For a cohesive look, use a limited number of colours—creamware as the predominant collection, for example, with a few accents in another colour.
- Setting the table with your best china just looks too staged for my liking. Stick with a centrepiece of fresh flowers or graceful candlesticks.

Bath
- Fill a basket with spa treatments such as soaps, lotions and jars of facial products. Hang one piece of art, create good storage and clear counters of clutter except for a vase with flowers.

Bedroom
- Keep your dresser clear of items. Place creams and lotions in a basket—better yet, store them in the bathroom. At one open house I saw, the 30 bottles of perfume on the dresser were more reminiscent of a bordello than the soothing retreat it could have been.
- Two lamps on either end of a dresser will give a symmetrical dressed-up look, and add to the lighting scheme.
- Plump up the bed with lots of pillows.
- On the bedside table keep items to a

minimum—a lamp, an alarm clock, a book and a photograph.

· White bed linens are the best route in any staged home—they read crisp and clean, reflect more light and work with any décor. In a child's room, however, this rule is meant to be broken—bring on the colour. Hot pink and lime green for girls, and navy, red and tan for boys.

Bookshelves and other display shelves

· Remove dust jackets on books to show the non-clashing cloth binding; cover certain types in white paper; arrange horizontally and vertically, prop things on top, like wood candle-sticks, etc.

· Balance colour: if the shelves are white, don't fill with creamware, but a combination of books stacked lying down or upright, vases in darker colours and metal objects. Creamware shows up nicely, though, on dark wood shelves. If your bookshelves are white, and you have glass to show off, display those items in front of books or a wooden box so they stand out. Vary the texture of things on the shelves.

· Consider placing a small lamp on one of the shelves. Or rig up disposable lighting strips tucked under the shelf overhang to add illumination.

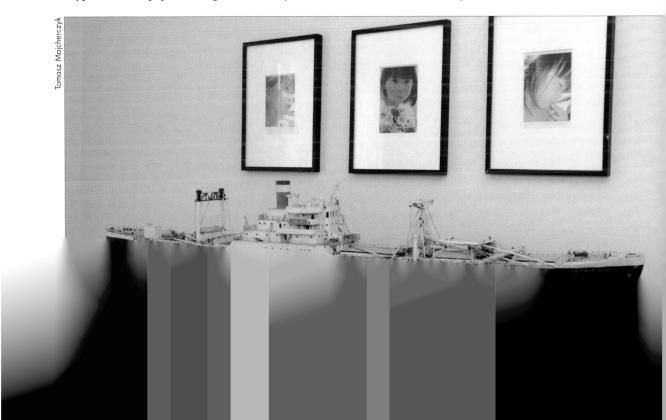

Tomasz Majcherczyk

· Don't fill your bookshelves only with books. Give some breathing space by adding some art objects. This is also where you can mingle your smaller accessories—it's the element of surprise that works on a bookshelf because you don't expect to see a little bronze figure or a silver flask. On top of stacked books, place small, decorative storage boxes, framed photos, a piece of coral, shell or pottery; place small pieces of art against the back of the shelf.

· Place a vertical stack of books on a shelf next to a wooden box, or next to a plate or small framed artwork on top of horizontally stacked books. Try a zigzag approach to the little pockets of space between books where objects will be—some decorators suggest a Z-shape, but I think that looks too forced. A random zigzag of objects, and books with colourful jackets, keeps the eye moving. It shows this is a home people have enjoyed.

Trim and details

· Solid wood doors, baseboards and trim are details people love. If you don't have them, but have the time, add them. Crown moulding is easy to add, but can overwhelm a really small room.

· Update hardware in your kitchen and bath.

Mirrors

· Can be used especially where you don't have a window. Get an old window, paint it white and have it fitted with mirrored glass to create a window where you don't have one.

· A mirror over the mantel expands space and reflects light. Go one step further by lighting candles in front of it, especially if they're housed in clear glass vases or hurricane shades.

· Hang mirrors where they can reflect light and a view. You want to highlight attractive areas, so place near a window that gets lots of sun. Be sure that any reflected view is an attractive one.

· Find large frames at garage sales and thrift stores—usually they're gaudy and finished with bright gold paint, and lots of filigree embellishments. Paint cream white, celadon green, or blue—whatever matches your décor—and fit with mirrored glass.

· A large floor-to-ceiling mirror propped on the wall opposite a window reflects the outdoors and creates the illusion of even more windows.

Artwork

You may want to rehang your art. Chances are very good it's hung either too high, too low, or on a wall that's not right for it—even experienced designers get it wrong. Start by taking everything off the walls, separating into two groups—what you love, and what you'd rather stick in storage. Group same-size pieces and arrange them on the floor before you hammer in the nails. Keep in mind coloration as well—and what will show up well against what wall colour.

Place artwork at eye level. The exception is a

double-height space, where you should try an abstract that is very large, or a tapestry, and hang it above the five-foot mark. Frame using a mat that's within the colour family of the art itself, or pure white—the mat allows for breathing room between the frame and the piece of art.

It's all right to hang art lower than eye level if it means creating a connection to the furniture. Art can draw the eye around the room. Arrange in triangles, with art over the sofa connecting to other objects on an end table, for instance.

Less is more, especially when each piece is large. Displaying a few larger pieces makes more of an impact, and draws the eye without cluttering the visual landscape of your home. Let the pieces of art you choose stand out, rather than choosing them to match the furniture.

Instead of hanging pictures, lean them against the wall on the floor, or along a narrow shelf. They don't even need to be framed if the look you're aiming for is slightly bohemian.

Shelves for artwork and display look best when they're built to fit the room's architecture, installed wall to wall rather than floating in the middle of the wall. Install on their own or as a series of shelves, but the size should fit the scale of the room, and should be compatible with other details such as baseboards and window and door trim.

Family photographs are fine, but limit the numbers. Candid shots, either black and white or colour, in large enough frames, can make quite an impact. But restrict them to retreat areas—bedrooms and family rooms—rather than living or dining areas.

Flowers

· Place fresh sprigs in tin cans, or anything cylindrical, and tie two of them together with raffia.
· Arrange a terra cotta pot, with crocus, ivy and candles.
· Place tulips in a vase with the stems cut short enough that the blooms come just to the top of the vase, but not over the edge. To keep cut tulips fresh longer, put pennies in the bottom of the vase.
· Amaryllis and other bulbs can be forced indoors during colder months.
· If the vase is larger at the top than the bottom, tie the base of the bouquet together with twine and allow the blooms to spill out over the top.
· Ginger jars, no matter how long they've been around, are pretty vases for a mantel.
· Fresh flowers, or fresh fruit (such as lemons in a bowl) look good and make a house feel like a home. A bowl of oranges in a crystal bowl on the dining room table gives a fresh scent and burst of colour.

CHAPTER 9
CURB APPEAL *First Impressions Last Forever*

Agents would say that curb appeal is so important that buyers know within a few minutes of driving by whether they even want to step foot inside. On an intuitive level, buyers can extrapolate a lot about what a house is like inside by what they see on the outside. Is the front of the house clean, freshly painted, tidy, in good repair? Those are the signs that make buyers want to see more, and that will prime them to have their hopes confirmed. So before you put up that "For Sale" sign, you'll want to do whatever you can to send the right message to every prospective buyer who drives by or comes up your walk.

Front walk

Make an entrance that will get you noticed. Draw the eye to the front door with urns lining the steps, or colourful bedding plants lining the walkway. There are literally dozens of ways to make the entrance more attractive and inviting, including a flagstone walkway, new steps, stone planters, a

stone bench, a new mailbox (or fresh paint on the old one).

Garden

Remove dead or struggling plants, and consider bordering your front yard with new shrubs. Add new plantings to fill in bare patches, or fill in the empty spots in a garden with a layer of pine bark mulch. Black or cream urns, planted with quick-blooming flowers, are an instant makeover. In the winter, plant them with boxwoods (if you can get your hands on them) and place them here and there for architectural interest.

Sparkly lights in a topiary or bushes are festive at any time of year. Statuary, too, has immediate appeal when placed in unexpected spots in the garden. Solar lamps immediately convey the sense of a well-tended garden, and light up when buyers come to see the house at night. Spotlights strategically placed behind plants (or in front) can add drama to the front of the house at night.

Steve Leach

Exterior walls

Reinvigorate chipped, peeling or dated paint with a fresh exterior coat. For colour choices, head to your favourite paint company's colour-coordinated selection sheet for exteriors. Strong contrasts between the house, trim and doors make a house look smaller and more chopped up. As in the interior, use two colours from the same family for both trim and exterior (wood, aluminum siding,

stucco, etc.), then add a punchy accent colour for the front door and shutters. It makes sense to coordinate your colours with your neighbour's exterior, as long as it still goes with the cladding on your own house.

I've seen many small, drab homes come alive with a coat of paint on the brick. But while painting exterior brick may be a fast, effective outdoor makeover, it must be done properly, by prepping the surface first, and using the right paint (consult a reputable paint dealer on best ways to do this).

Front door and windows

Refurbishing your front door with a fresh coat of paint is usually the best and most cost-effective option. If your front door has seen better days and can't be brought back to life, replace it with a new, sturdy door. Remove the storm door to help the front door stand out more. The garage door should be painted neutral—rather than with the punchy accent—to blend with the house.

In addition to polishing the door brasses, make sure the door opens and closes properly: no sticking, no forcing the latch to make it hold. Make sure the doorbell works. Get a new doormat, but refrain from buying one with a cute saying.

Adding shutters may enhance your windows, depending on the style of your house. As stated in a previous chapter, clean windows are critical, and will repay you many times over for the time you put in!

Porch

Paint the railings and floor of the porch a colour that will complement the exterior cladding.

Nothing beats a summer evening on the front porch, so create an atmosphere of quiet celebration that will have prospective buyers imagining the easy life in their new home. Hang a real candelabra over the seating area, for example, and arrange a small table and a few chairs on a rug of seagrass, coir, sisal, or a beach mat made of woven grass. Arrange porch furniture for easy conversation and to take advantage of any view you might have. Add a lamp if you've got an exterior outlet close enough. Hang wind chimes for pleasant sounds to greet people.

Accessorize the porch, just as you would any other room in the house. The idea is to expand your living space as much as possible so buyers will be amazed by how big the house is. Display architectural fragments such as old iron grates and weather vanes, or rustic items such as duck decoys on walls or shelves—but in moderation. Bring books, flowers and accessories out of doors. A wicker or iron trunk works well as a coffee table. Porch swings, plumped up with cushions in colours that complement the house colour, are irresistible. Potted plants can add texture to a porch, especially when grouped together.

Maintenance, cleaning and safety

Front steps slippery? Paint steps first, allow to dry, and then create a template for "traction strips" by outlining with painter's tape. In a new container, add a little sand to the paint (you can use beach sand that's been sifted through a sieve to remove leaves and pebbles) in proportions of two cups of paint to three-quarters cup of sand. Paint inside the template blocks, stirring the paint continuously.

Extend your gaze beyond the lot line and try to keep the street clean of garbage—within reason. Report abandoned cars. Cut the lawn of the neighbours on either side, if you must. It will show your house to advantage. Tactfully offer to clean up the neighbour's yard—the Beverley Hillbillies may have been fun to watch on TV but no one wants to buy next door to them. Keep your car clean, and park extra cars away from the house.

Consider getting a cedar storage bin to hide your garbage and recycling containers out of sight. Ensure that all exterior light fixtures are in working order, with functioning light bulbs. Make sure all outside elements are spotless.

Garage

This must be kept as clean as the interior of the house. Storage should be neat and not entirely filled up. There should be space to actually park the car. If you've been storing all your stuff here for the past 10 years, rent a locker and stow the stuff there instead.

Below: There's just enough seclusion for this brick house that the yellow front door stands out just enough for a little contrast.

Steve Leach

CHAPTER 10

THE BACK YARD *Creating the Outdoor Room*

Weary urbanites, thirsty for space to relax and entertain, are turning to the last urban frontier—the "outdoor room" situated beyond the back door. Identified by real estate analysts and trend-watchers alike as the place most likely to increase your home's resale value, the outdoor room extends living space for less cost than adding onto the house.

Nora Lukss' modern, airy multi-level house, for example, is in an area dominated by traditional homes—Arts and Crafts, two-storey brick Victorians and rambling cottages. Her first attempt to sell was unsuccessful, though the home's interior was bright and well furnished. So Nora, a certified designer, pulled out all her tools, and turned her attention to the back yard.

She designed a series of rooms: the triangular deck of the front "room" just off the kitchen got a fresh coat of paint, black urns filled with geraniums and a teak chair and table; a middle "room" was created with a stone slab floor, canvas gazebo and dining table and chairs; while the sunny spot in the very back of the garden got a layer of pine bark mulch and two teak loungers. It took only two weekends for Nora's husband, Al, to complete the project—and he lost weight doing it!

The house sold in a week—and the new owners asked to buy all the outdoor furnishings. The moral of the story is: ignore the back yard at your peril.

Start with a design that mirrors a house with halls (pathways), walls (hedges, fences) and various rooms designated for separate functions. Think about how the garden might be used—a spot for entertaining, for lounging and relaxing, for eating, for grilling, and figure out the most logical place for those to take place. For example, the grill should be close enough to dining for convenience, but not so close that it blows smoke in people's eyes. Work with the yard's natural topography—sloping yards might benefit from tiered seating or eating areas, or raised rock-garden beds.

There's lots of help available, in books, magazines and online. The website for *Better Homes and*

Gardens has several garden plans to get ideas from. Go to www.bhg.com, click on garden, and search garden plans. Building supply stores regularly hold DIY workshops on gardening elements from stone paver paths to retaining walls.

If full landscaping is not in your budget or schedule, follow the French: they seem to be able to create a welcoming garden in the most uninviting places, with little more than a quirky collection of pots and containers. Every shape and size can be grouped in nooks and filled with bright annuals—impatiens and cyclamens in the shade, and geraniums and pansies in the sun. As inside, pare back, edit and don't overdo the containers or it will look like a jumble instead of the charming spot in Provence you intended.

Containers can also be hung overhead, from the house's soffits or eaves, or along the deck and porch railings, which gives a great view from either side of the railing. For staging, stick with a restrained colour scheme that complements your home. For yellow brick houses, baskets of blue or purple flowers are gorgeous; for red or brown brick, choose white or pink and glossy green.

It doesn't take much time, money or energy to create atmosphere—even the tiniest spot can be improved with a table and chair, and set apart from the rest of the yard by loosely set flagstone pavers.

A small condo balcony can be turned into a garden oasis with a banquette against the building's wall, a comfy lounge chair and a bistro table for seating. With a trellis on either end for privacy, new paint on the concrete floor and the exterior door, an electric water fountain for the soothing sound of gurgling water, and candles in lanterns, you're all set. Check with the condo rules first, though, to see if there are restrictions on what you can do.

Tiny urban yards make perfect Japanese gardens—especially since Japanese gardens don't require grass. All you need is a good design, pea gravel, stepping stones, a water feature and bushy green plants tucked in containers. Small ponds and other water features can be installed over a weekend. Then add wind chimes elsewhere in the garden.

If you're really on a limited—or nonexistent—timeline and budget, or a makeover is beyond your abilities, patience or desire, at the very least mow the lawn, rake the leaves, prune the bushes (or shovel the snow if it's winter). Sweep the porch, scrub the front door, polish the brass, make sure the house number is visible (better yet, change it, since they're inexpensive and easy to install) and stow the plastic trucks and backhoes. Hide the garbage and recycling bins. Weed the garden—it's amazing what a little dark earth can do to show off plants.

And bring on the paint—it's cheap. When fences, iron urns and wood containers are painted the same shade—green, black or brown—the look is simple, harmonious and consistent.

Below: Stager and designer Nora Lukss designed a back yard plan that was simple to execute, but added hugely to the overall look. Taking the narrow existing yard design she created three "rooms"—one for entertaining on the existing deck (by adding more flower containers), another for dining by adding a stone patio and gazebo, and the last for soaking up the sun by adding mulch floor and teak lounge chairs.

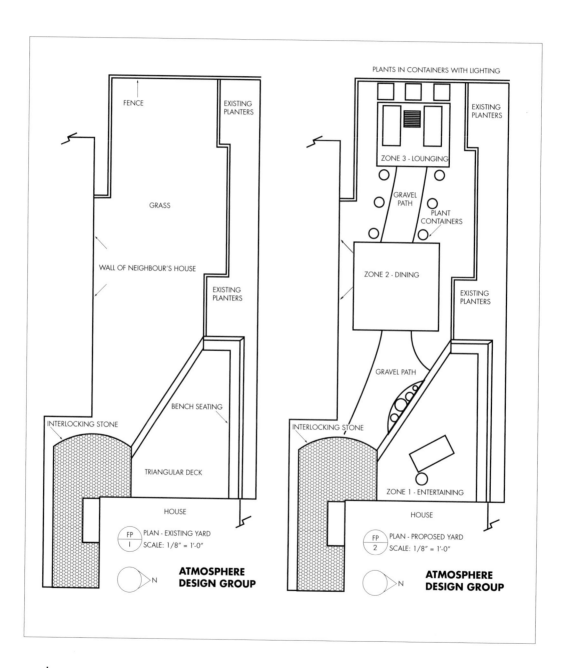

FENCE

EXISTING PLANTERS

GRASS

WALL OF NEIGHBOUR'S HOUSE

EXISTING PLANTERS

BENCH SEATING

INTERLOCKING STONE

TRIANGULAR DECK

HOUSE

FP 1 — PLAN - EXISTING YARD
SCALE: 1/8" = 1'-0"

N

ATMOSPHERE DESIGN GROUP

PLANTS IN CONTAINERS WITH LIGHTING

EXISTING PLANTERS

ZONE 3 - LOUNGING

GRAVEL PATH

PLANT CONTAINERS

ZONE 2 - DINING

EXISTING PLANTERS

GRAVEL PATH

INTERLOCKING STONE

ZONE 1 - ENTERTAINING

HOUSE

FP 2 — PLAN - PROPOSED YARD
SCALE: 1/8" = 1'-0"

N

ATMOSPHERE DESIGN GROUP

Floors

· Consider outdoor paving—bricks, flagstones, tiles or large cement slabs—the same as you would indoor flooring. A change in flooring material or the direction in which the flooring is laid helps define distinct and separate areas such as dining and sunbathing.

· Paving stones keep the yard free of mud, and looking trim and tidy. If you don't like the hard edge of paving materials, consider softening it by growing herbs between flagstones, or laying down cedar mulch or pea gravel.

· Pea gravel is a great choice for paths because it requires almost no maintenance or watering, only needs raking into place every now and again, is fairly inexpensive, always dry, and the crunch underfoot adds a pleasurable sound to the garden. (Even the dog's business is easy to pick up on pea gravel.)

· A garden path is fairly easy to make. Level the ground by digging down about two inches, line the sides with garden hose or tape, and pour bags of pea gravel into place. Make your path wind through the garden so that it seems to enlarge the space and the experience of moving through it. Create points of interest such as statuary, gazing balls or birdhouses, which can be especially eye-catching when on a pedestal. Statuary that's partially concealed by greenery evokes a sense of mystery, especially when you come upon it at the end of a path.

· Lanterns and torches are good for general lighting and a walkway lined with solar-powered lamps provides evening drama.

Walls

· Garden walls, usually boring expanses of pressure-treated wood, get a new lease on life with trellis, climbers and even wall fountains. Plant climbers along the trellis, and vary the heights for a more natural look. If you're short on time, hang strings of small electric lights for a glittery, glam look at night.

· Raised beds can act as "room dividers" in an open space. Trellis also works well as a divider and provides vertical elements in an otherwise horizontal space.

· Hang a mirror at the back of a short, square yard to expand the vista.

· Lattice is the best invention since sliced bread. It comes pre-made, you can stain or paint it (though you don't have to), it allows more light than a regular fence, it's cheaper and quicker to install, and it improves air circulation through the garden.

· An even cheaper solution for privacy is bamboo poles or fencing stuck directly into the ground along your property line. This really quick makeover is especially effective if you have a semi-detached house and need to obstruct an unsightly mess on the other side of the fence.

Outdoor maintenance

· Rent a power-washer. You won't believe how clean your deck, porch, siding and windows will be after using it. Agent Joy Verde says washing windows is the best—and cheapest—way to improve a house. Once everything is clean, decide what, if anything, needs painting.

· Make sure there are no burnt-out bulbs in your exterior lighting.

· Make sure there's a good spot for tools and garden equipment—many men make a beeline for the outdoor gadgets.

· If there's a little shed in the garden, give it a fresh coat of paint and decorate with window boxes and flowers.

· Repair and clean gutters.

· Keep plants from blocking windows. You want to see the house from the outside, and you want to be able to see the view from the inside. Remove dead plants and shrubs.

· Windex Outdoor cleaner can hook right onto a garden hose for cleaning without having to dry windows or climb a single rung of a ladder.

Furniture

· Thanks to new weatherproof materials, you can use almost any furniture outdoors. A spray can of rustproof paint covers frames, while Sunbrella fabrics handle the upholstery.

· Bright pillows make even the plainest wood bench an inviting spot to sit.

· Paint any metal outdoor chairs with Tremclad rust paint; you can even paint your plastic chairs in bright bold colours with Tremclad plastic resin paint (Rust-Oleum paint for plastic). Linens 'n Things has a line of resin Muskoka chairs in wonderfully bright colours (teal blue, hot pink and acid green).

Quick Tips

· Pull up two lounge chairs on either side of a small table, and fill an urn with a summer arrangement of annuals.

· There's nothing quite like a hammock to telegraph that this is a place to hang out and relax without a care in the world. If you don't have trees on which to suspend the hammock, get a hammock with a stand.

· A narrow strip at the side of the house becomes an inviting pathway when set with square pavers on the diagonal and pea gravel in between.

· Rather than just a table and chairs plonked down under a cloth gazebo, make your outdoor dining room an event. Suspend a chandelier over the table, plugged in to an exterior electrical outlet. Or, if that can't be arranged, hang a glass votive pendant with a large candle (but not too close to the ceiling, for fire hazard reasons). Set the table with place mats and summery tableware.

· Arrange containers in a cozy spot, then work driftwood, rocks, moss and burlap into the "landscape" to make it look as though the plants are in a gorgeous bed rather than in containers.

CHAPTER 11

KITCHENS AND BATHS *The Working Heart of the Home*

Kitchens

Nothing animates home and family like food. We need it to survive, and to celebrate daily rituals. It's said that if all is well with the food—and the kitchen—a house comes alive.

While kitchens may be the heart of your home, they're also the heart of your investment. Today's super-savvy consumers have been fed on a steady diet of granite counters, custom cabinetry, double wall ovens, six-burner stoves and limestone floors from model homes, television shows and shelter magazines.

It's raised the expectation levels considerably, but since you're just staging your home, you're not likely to have the time, money or inclination to go for a full kitchen renovation costing tens of thousands of dollars. Don't despair—there are still lots of improvements you can make.

If the basic cabinetry and layout are good, but tired or dated, you can have the cabinets refaced—that is, have new doors put on existing cabinetry

boxes. Or you can leave the cabinets and install new floors and counters. Even getting a more updated laminate counter may be enough for the wow factor you need.

Other easy upgrades include: painting existing cabinets and walls, changing hardware, adding new sink and faucets, hanging new window treatments or having none at all; updating the lighting, and adding light to the underside of upper cabinets.

And, as with any room in a staged house, decluttering is key. Store all small appliances out of sight—that gorgeous electric-blue KitchenAid mixer may be okay to leave on display, but stow the grimy toaster oven, blender, coffee grinder, and so on. Also remove *all* magnets and children's art from the door of the fridge and store dish racks, soap containers and vegetable brushes out of sight.

Cabinets

Cabinetry is the biggest part of the kitchen, so spend what time and money you have here. In some cases, you can get away with existing cabinetry, and blow the budget on granite counters and new appliances!

But if the layout is a problem, you may have to start from scratch unless you can get away with moving things around. Remove any cabinets that impede the visual or physical flow of the space—hard-to-reach cabinets above a peninsula are a perfect example. Removing them altogether will reduce storage, but it will also make the space lighter and airier—always a bonus in staging. If floor space and layout allow, you may be able to compensate for lost space by adding the cabinets to the back side of the island or peninsula and topping the whole unit with an enlarged counter.

Islands rank high on the list of must-haves. Don't have one? If you have the space, ready-made islands can create the same look for a lot less—a rolling cart with butcher block top, or a harvest table that doubles as breakfast table and homework spot will do the trick.

If the layout is good and cabinets are in sound condition, you can update and upgrade them, with some of the following:

· Replace upper cabinet doors with new doors inset with frosted glass (check with the manufacturer, or see if in-stock cabinets will match). Alternatively, remove the doors altogether and leave the open shelving for displaying your best dishes. This works especially well with rustic or country looks.

Paint the interiors a complementary shade.
· Remove one upper in a long line of cabinets, add shelves painted the same colour as the walls (or cabinets) and display cookbooks or crockery. This gives essential visual breathing space and frees up counter space below.
· Update by adding moulding to plain wooden cupboard doors—it's fairly easy to install. Then paint over and even finish with a coat of antiquing glaze for old-world charm.
· It's possible to paint veneer and metal cabinets with the right products. (See Resources at the back of the book.) Laminate cabinets, too, if they're truly hideous and nothing else will tone them down, can be painted; if they're white and in good shape, painting may not be worthwhile for resale. Add a new counter, flooring and hardware for an updated look.

The key to success is carving out enough time to do the job properly, being patient and doing a proper prep job.

Replacing counters

Replacing or renewing counters is a quick update—because the surface is so large, it's the first thing you see.

Granite is fast becoming an industry standard, but it's expensive (though not as expensive as it used to be) and not all granites are created equal. It, or another solid surface material, are the only ones to consider, though, if your house is listed at a higher price point. Granites run between $60 and $120 a square foot, although you can sometimes get lucky finding granite counters at ReStore.

If the kitchen suffers from a bad layout and cabinets in awful shape, even granite counters won't save it. My neighbours installed $8,000 worth of granite in a 20-year-old kitchen, and would have been much further ahead rethinking the space.

Solid surface engineered quartz is a good compromise—pricier than laminate, and only marginally cheaper than granite (between $65 and $100 a square foot), it has granite's high-quality looks and durability.

Corian is another good choice, ranging between laminate and granite (at about $50 to $100 a square foot). It's a solid surface—made from plastic and minerals—and comes in a huge range of colours and patterns. Seams are invisible, scratches can be polished out with fine sandpaper—the downside is you can't put a hot pot on it without the risk of damage.

You'll find solid surface countertops with brand names such as Corian, Swanstone and Avonite. These counters are custom made and fit for your kitchen so you get a groutless, seamless look, in a variety of colours and styles. In my opinion, Corian just doesn't look as nice as true natural stones, but some people love it. Is granite better than Corian? Corian is durable, allowing scratches to be sanded out, but it cannot stand up to heat the way granite can (it claims to be safe up to 200° Fahrenheit, but they still recommend using a trivet for hot pans). How much does Corian cost? Less expensive than granite, it is still considerably more than tile to have made and installed in a kitchen or bathroom. Corian comes in more than 100 colours and is nonporous, so stains and spills wipe right off. Corian can be cut, routed, drilled, sculpted, bent or worked like a fine wood. Also, Corian does not require special sealants (remember, unlike even granite, which must be sealed every couple of years, it is non-porous!).

Opinion is divided on laminate. Many consider it old style, but I will happily defend it—it's long-lasting (my 12-year-old counter is virtually damage free), there are so many new patterns, such as faux stainless or hand-hammered copper, which are exquisite. You can also get interesting edges: the traditional bullnose; a squared-off edge that looks more like solid surface; and wood edge that gives a beautiful custom look.

Plus it costs as little as $15 a linear foot ($30 a linear foot installed). The difference between linear and square feet is that linear is measured for the length of the two-foot-deep counter, whereas square footage is measured by the overall surface—for example a 10-foot run of counter, two feet deep, would be 20 square feet, not 10 linear feet.

Imaginahome Inc., Tomasz Majcherczyk

Going right over existing laminate is another option, either with 4-inch by 4-inch tiles, and a bullnose tile, or with larger granite tiles (about one-quarter the cost of a straight run of granite). There's also a new product called Granite Transformations, which is a thin piece of granite, cut to fit right over the existing counter.

I've seen people experiment with ceramic tile as a counter—it looks nice, especially the natural stone tile—but in the long run, it's more difficult to keep the grout lines clean. Ceramic also comes in a range of sizes (from small glass mosaics to large 12-inch tiles, but for counters the 4-inch to 6-inch range is best. The materials range from plain and simple porcelain to imitation travertine, limestone (which stains) and granite. The price range is wide but usually reasonable (4-inch by 4-inch tiles can be as low as 50¢), though labour costs can be high unless you do it yourself. For the time and trouble, new laminate is probably a better choice.

Mixing counter materials is fine depending on where they are. For a snack station next to the fridge, solid wood works (IKEA has seven-foot beech and oak counters for $90). This wouldn't work near the sink, although at that price it could easily be replaced.

Polished concrete is another product that's gaining popularity, especially in modern settings with an industrial or loft aesthetic. Concrete counters are poured in place, so they can be made to fit anywhere, in a variety of profiles, thicknesses and tints. Before you use them, however, be sure that your target market is sufficiently design conscious to appreciate your choice.

Backsplash

Removing old backsplash is a big messy deal, so unless the tiles are cracked or truly hideous, avoid it.

To start with, thoroughly clean the backsplash tiles and the grout. If grout needs replacing, it's a fairly easy DIY job. What's tricky is matching the grout colour. First you clean the grout area with vinegar and water, then use a grout saw to remove the damaged grout. Dampen joints with water and mop up with paper towel. Mix compound and apply with a grout float, filling the joints, then smooth the surface with a rounded stick (from the hardware store) and remove excess with a sponge or squeegee.

In areas where you want to add or replace the backsplash, and there's no chance that water will come into contact with the areas you have in mind, consider applying "beadboard" wallpaper or a photocopied piece of art to the wall and then applying some serious coats of polyurethane as a protective finish. Even crackle it for an authentic mural look.

Flooring

If you have ceramic floors, it's easier to change the elements around them—such as painting cabinets or changing the countertop—than trying to rip up the tiles. If they're in very bad shape, though, you may have no choice.

What you can put over the existing floor depends on what's down there now. Vinyl floors are easy to remove and replace. Linoleum tiles need to be removed as well before putting something else down, although some floating floors (laminates) can be installed over anything. If the underlying floor is in bad shape, though, flaws will telegraph over time. Some new laminates are stunning and cannot be distinguished from the real McCoy—like the snap-and-click faux slate boards that I currently have my eye on. But where it requires a new subfloor—replacing vinyl with ceramic requires ¾-inch plywood, as opposed to ¼-inch—you're adding significantly to the cost. But if you're installing ceramic where there used to be vinyl, keep in mind that you need a sufficiently thick plywood subfloor (at least ¾-inch as opposed to ¼-inch; ⅝-inch is even better).

For staging you want big bang for small bucks, so a floating vinyl floor would work best. Another option might be industrial rubber flooring— durable, easy underfoot, and can be installed floating over just about any floor—though it's a look that seems to fit better with modern interiors. (Check out Armstrong.com, tarkett-floors.com and Dupont.com for some incredible faux stone floors.)

Hardware

Changing hardware is an easy way to update a kitchen. While new hardware comes in a variety of beautiful styles, lean toward plain rather than trendy for staging purposes—they're cheaper and appeal to more tastes. Hardware can be found at all big box stores, as well as at IKEA (but check measurements because not all handles are the same).

Coordinate hardware finish with the sink and faucet to unify the kitchen. Don't be cheap! Good hardware can be expensive, but will dramatically alter the look.

Appliances

New or updated appliances go a long way to updating a kitchen. If cabinets are sound and layout is pleasing, it might be smarter to upgrade with new stainless steel appliances (which you also get to take away with you, or at least use as a negotiating tool). Barring that, consider paneling the appliance fronts—stainless or whatever matches the cabinets—to help everything blend, which is especially important in a small space. Always keep in mind the cost to update versus the price increase you're likely to realize from doing it: paneling the appliances may not be worthwhile if your home is in a neighbourhood that doesn't demand top dollar.

Invest in a new range hood, or better yet install one of the new space-saver microwaves above the range with a built-in fan.

Fixtures

Replacing the sink and faucet is an easy upgrade. If you have to take the sink out to replace the faucets, replace both, unless you have a good-quality stainless steel sink that cleans up well—why spend another $100 to $300 (or more) if you don't have to?

Faucets can be purchased from any hardware store, big box or otherwise, IKEA, Canadian Tire or Zellers. Check out restaurant supply stores, too, since you can sometimes get faucets cheaper and in styles you might not find at the standard box stores.

Lighting

Large windows and natural light are wonderful, so be sure to enhance them with the right kind of window coverings. Roman blinds or wood blinds are best bets in kitchens because they're neat, trim and not grease catchers the way panels are. Personally, I prefer no curtains for unimpeded light and view.

If your kitchen isn't bright enough, expand your existing track lighting or add new. The kitchen table or an island can be highlighted with pendant lights in a trendy nickel finish.

Strip lights or uplights on top of cabinets will bring that dead zone to life. Easily installed under-cabinet lighting casts an interesting light on counters and gives the whole kitchen a serene glow after dark. See the chapter on lighting for more ideas.

Staging the Eating Areas

If you're lucky enough to have an eat-in kitchen, make sure the table has an element of display. A full china setting isn't necessary, but at least a centrepiece. That can range from fresh flowers in a simple vase to a hurricane glass over a pillar candle. With no eat-in kitchen, create a connection between the kitchen and dining room through colour, finishes and style. If the dining room feels too formal, tone it down with sisal carpet, bamboo place mats and an informal centrepiece.

If you don't already have one, is there anywhere to carve out a breakfast nook? Can you build in a banquette against the wall (or get an old church pew), then add a narrow refectory table and bench on the opposite side? Plush stuffed cushions will make it very comfy especially if it overlooks the back yard. Even a fold-down table can be attached to a wall or the end run of the cabinets to create a breakfast nook.

Furniture

Freestanding furniture can save a kitchen from looking cold or utilitarian. Choose a "statement piece," displayed with beautiful objects but completely free of clutter. (For tips on display see Chapter 8.) For a country look, use blue milk paint on an old jam cupboard, or milky green or yellow on a harvest table.

No island? Create one with a small antique table topped by butcher block, granite or marble. You can often find slabs of marble or granite at salvage yards, which regularly remove this kind of stuff from old banks.

If there's a lot of furniture—like the nine-piece dining room suite my husband insisted on buying—pare back by moving some pieces to other rooms, or storing it. All you need in a dining room is a table and chairs, and a place to store dishes.

Walls

Since there's so little wall space in a kitchen, you can afford to be bold with colour: eggplant, tangerine, lime, cherry, chocolate (all food colours, incidentally). But keep in mind the colours of your cabinets, appliances and display dishes—as well as the general colour scheme of your whole home.

Although the kitchen is a natural place to hang things on walls, resist and desist! Take off all those S-hooks, spatulas, spoons and burnt copper-bottom pots and store them out of sight. Ditto for the dried herbs hanging from the rafters.

If yours is a family-friendly neighbourhood (and you have children of your own), you can create a kid area in the kitchen—chalk paint on a wall, framed with a shelf and hooks—which doubles as a message centre or meal-planning area for the adults.

Accessories

Add your personality to the kitchen with collections, baskets, pretty bottles of vinegar and gleaming copper pots, but only if they're in good shape and you abide by the rule of moderation in all things.

In front of a plain window, create some interest with glass shelving. Glass jars containing beans and lentils, or potted herbs, give welcome texture and colour.

Since kitchens have a lot of hard surfaces, take the opportunity to add texture with wood flooring (or wood-look laminate), fabric valance or Roman blinds at the window, and an area rug or runner. Display bright-coloured cookbooks, art, ceramics or dishes. Fresh flowers and herbs add colour and scent.

While the space above the upper cabinets is tempting to "display" your finest, there's a reason it's called the dead zone—it takes years to get up there and retrieve the stuff. Remove it: the clutter just closes in the room. The only acceptable thing up there *might* be a row of identical wicker baskets to hide stuff in a neat and orderly way.

Bathrooms

Kitchen and baths are where most buyers pay special attention.

Several years ago while producing segments for a home décor TV show, I orchestrated a tiny bathroom makeover. It was simple but dramatic: just by changing to a new pedestal sink and shower curtain, and beefing up the stock of creams, lotions and towels made it an inviting spa retreat.

The cheapest—and maybe the best—way to update the bath is to clean it thoroughly. Nothing impresses quite like a spotlessly clean bathroom with sparkling fixtures and blindingly white tile grout. Declutter by clearing off counters and sink edges and corral all your toiletries into plastic bins inside the vanity, or in a storage unit such as a pretty glass-fronted étagère above the toilet or a freestanding floor unit. (You can find them everywhere in big box stores, Canadian Tire, HomeSense, IKEA, Zellers, etc.) Or store your stuff elsewhere and leave the space clear altogether.

Most buyers have quite enough work on their hands running a household, two jobs, children, and so on, and even the simple task of replacing a washer in a dripping faucet will take on Herculean proportions in their minds. So fix all those annoying small repairs such as leaks in showers or from toilet seals, cracked grout, loose fixtures, old and dated towel bars.

Tiles and Grout

Clean tiles and grout thoroughly in the shower stall and on the floor, using vinegar or products specially designed to remove mildew, lime and scale. If noticeable stains remain, regrout around the tiles of the shower and the floor. If the floor is vinyl tile, replace anything cracked, peeling or loose, or install new vinyl sheet floor over everything. There are tons of options in vinyl.

If you are installing new tiles and it's a small room, lay tiles on the diagonal to widen and open the room. Laying tiles this way will require more than the actual square footage, but the results are worth it.

Tub

A claw-foot tub has classic lines. If you have one, play it up with a tub tray and soaps, and a thick shower curtain if you've got a shower ring around the top. Automotive wax will restore the lustrous shine of the tub's interior, as long as the porcelain is intact (you can do small touch-ups with special paint purchased from the hardware store). Paint the exterior in a fashion-forward colour (deep moss, warm putty brown, baby blue, taupe pink), as long as it complements the look of the bathroom and the rest of the house.

Shower

Clean, fix, renew or replace all grout. If you have old sliding doors on the tub or surrounding the shower, consider replacing them with frameless glass—it visually expands the space and gives it a luxury, updated feeling.

Below: : Because repairs needed to be done behind the toilet in this bathroom, and the beige tiles couldn't be matched, stager Bruno Billio suggested painting the lower tiles in a white paint specially made for tiles. This way they blend with the floor, and the upper tiles act as a bridge between floor and wall colour.

Toilet

Replace the toilet seat—a new one is sparkling clean and makes the whole room look new.

Sink

Pedestal sinks look great but provide absolutely no storage, so if you have one of these make sure there are enough towel bars to hold lots of the thick and thirsty stuff. A pretty storage unit beside the sink takes up little space and stores most of the essentials. On the top, display a vase of fresh flowers or an art object. Sometimes a pedestal sink is the best choice in a small bathroom because it increases negative space (empty space) around objects, making the room feel more spacious.

If the vanity needs replacing, shop around for a new one that looks like furniture, and in a wood veneer that matches the rest of the house—beech, wenge wood, maple. You can find these practically everywhere.

Fixtures

Refurbish or replace any fixtures that look a little worse for wear—including the toilet roll holder. (If you worry about drilling holes in the walls, get a stainless holder that sits on the floor.) Original chrome hardware and fixtures eventually get worn, but are easily re-chromed if time or budget permit. If not, buy new. A towel rack on the back of the door saves space.

Tomasz Majcherczyk

Consider, if necessary, replacing shower bars and faucets. Stainless is the "gold standard" these days, but if you have perfectly good brass fixtures and replacing them will be expensive, just polish them up, and choose a wall colour and shower curtain that will tone them down. Some colours that work with brass include chocolate, taupe, copper, ecru, sand, smoke grey, seagreen and olive.

Storage

Everyone needs storage, especially in bathrooms, so clean out the shelves (see Chapter 3 for advice on purging) and install shelves if necessary and possible. Consider adding extra glass shelves inside medicine cabinets (can be cut at hardware stores), but keep the display minimal.

Open shelves should be stripped of the bulky jars of cosmetics and hair products, and lined instead with matching spa-like glass containers (see Resources at back of book) for makeup pads, cotton balls, Q-tips, etc. Or corral into a new storage unit above the toilet (remember to allow enough space below it for the toilet lid to open and shut).

Unless you're one of the few lucky ones to have a laundry facility in your second-floor bathroom, relocate that space-hogging laundry hamper by installing individual laundry bags in the bedroom closets. Alternatively, get everyone in the daily habit of trotting their dirty clothes to the washer.

Curtains: shower and window

Drapery can be a challenge. For a small bathroom, Roman blinds are the best bet. Trim and neat, they don't visually intrude; you can find them ready made at IKEA and Zellers, among other stores. Wood blinds are also good choices, but need to be water-resistant faux wood. Even a gauzy sheer drapery panel floating romantically to the floor is better than nothing.

When it comes to shower curtains, new is a good investment. Clear vinyl works best in a tiny bath because it permits sightlines through to the wall behind the tub and expands the space. On the other hand, fabric curtains can warm up a room, adding texture in a room with mostly cool hard surfaces, and lends a spa feel. Keep the curtains tied back to one side while showing, for greater openness. Haunt the sales bins at fabric and bed and bath outlets, and you'll find something inexpensive.

Walls and other structural things

Paint is the easiest way to update your bathroom. Since you can't change the tiles (it's not usually an investment on which you'll see an adequate return), select a colour that complements them. Green tiles, for example, can be toned down with cream or ecru walls for a real spa flavour (then add white and pale celery towels, mats, soaps and sea sponges, clear glass jars and pale sea-green lotions). With black-and-white tiles, try rose, buttercream, or deep sage walls, white towels and accessories, and a few hand towels in a two-tone jacquard to add a little colour. For my oyster-pink tiles, and white and rosy-taupe towels, the paint salesman picked out a milk chocolate colour. I was skeptical until it was on the walls.

If the bathroom is all white, either punch it up with clear, bold colours—yellow, red, green, blue and a touch of black—or go completely neutral with tone on tone, but add lots of textural layers with wicker baskets, sea sponges, natural accessories (driftwood, pumice stones, pebbles, etc.), as well as towels and mats in ecru, almond or biscuit colours.

Below: *Mirrors along one whole wall over this vanity add sparkle and expand the space, but you have to be careful of how much accessorizing, since the reflection will give you twice the amount. In this bathroom, stager Heather Shaw opted to go simple: white towels folded neatly, a simple white candle and a fresh white terry cloth shower curtain.*

Beadboard is a nice addition for just about any bathroom look, from country, to spa, to traditional, and it's quite easy to install. If you don't have the time to fiddle with it, though, consider the new beadboard wallpaper.

The Fun Stuff

Add new towels—you don't have to buy a whole set, just a few hand towels to complement the colour scheme. White is always a good choice, but for a little punch try some jacquard weave in white and the bathroom colour.

Simple neutrals are always good in the bath but there are exceptions to the rule: in my tiny,

windowless basement bathroom, where an angled shower jostles with a toilet and a half-vanity (salvaged from the upstairs bath, then cut in half to fit), vibrant colour was the only choice. With walls in buttery yellow, Mexican terra cotta floor tiles, backsplash tiles in a patterned Mexican blue, green, white and yellow, and a marine blue mirror, the best choice for towels was coral, navy and acid green.

Mirror, mirror

The mirror over the sink needs to be big, beautiful and clean. Although I prefer the clean look of an unframed bevelled mirror with sparkling chrome fixtures, a plain bathroom would do well with

some small charming details, such as framing the bathroom mirror with a picture frame, picked up from a flea market, garage sale, thrift store, painted and hung directly on the wall. Or you can buy a big baroque highly detailed mirror from one of the big box stores, give it a coat of oil-based paint and hang it over the sink—inexpensive and beautiful.

Lighting

Although lighting on either side of the mirror is the most flattering, a new fixture over the sink is better than nothing. If it's old, or really dated (think makeup strip lighting à la 1970), replace it with one of the many inexpensive options from builder stores. As one stager cautioned, though, buyers are very familiar with big box store fare, so if your home is high end, shop at a higher-end lighting store. You can save money by checking out the clearance items—stager Heather Shaw picked up a beautiful modern chandelier for $150 (reduced from $450) at Union Lighting, an upscale lighting store in Toronto.

Tomasz Majcherczyk

CHAPTER 12
THE OTHER ROOMS *Separating the Public from the Private*

Although kitchens and baths may be a buyer's primary concern, the other rooms go a long way in creating the mood and lifestyle you need when selling your home.

Each room must read loud and clear what its function is—buyers who have to spend time figuring out the focus and function of a room get irritated. Generally speaking, no matter how you've been using the rooms in your house, it works better if rooms are restored to their intended use until the house is sold.

Foyer

The foyer, as transition point between outdoors and in, sets the tone for the whole house.

If you've been blessed with a large front hall, thank your lucky stars. A large gracious hall makes a significant introduction to your home, as well as provides room for storing mitts, scarves, hats and a place to drop keys and mail. This is a great place to create impact with a table in the centre and a

vase of fresh flowers or great piece of sculpture on top. A runner underneath adds warmth and visual interest.

With the trend to knocking down walls, the skinny hall is often a thing of the past. But sadly, the entry hall itself is also a thing of the past: in the rush to remove walls, renovators have also removed entryways. Sometimes you find yourself in the middle of the living room immediately on entering the front door. If that's the case, move the living room furniture in slightly so that there's room to create an entryway. There are plenty of creative options available to do this—a console table mounted to the wall can handle mail and keys, while a slim container underneath can hold umbrellas.

If there is no room for a front hall closet, consider adding iron coat hooks to the wall just inside the door.

Keep furniture slim lined to prevent bulky obstructions in the sightlines. A narrow bench, even a wall-mounted one, is all you need to put on

Rohan Laylor

intense with colour—there's less space to cover. Since there's less light in a hall, the lighting is important for illuminating tasks such as putting on coats and shoes, and to shine a light on your home.

If the hardwood floors in your entry are showing signs of wear and tear, consider a painted treatment. The practice of painting floors began in the 17th century with poor folk mimicking the parquet in European palaces by painting the pattern on their own plain floors. It soon became all the rage.

If you're creative and handy with a paintbrush, you could create a faux terra cotta tile, or a diamond pattern of two alternating colours. The diamond pattern, on the bias, in a narrow hall, has the effect of widening the space. You could also alternate painted squares with natural floor.

Above all, keep the front entry spotlessly clean, and walls and trim free of fingerprints.

Living Room

The living room is usually the place that we put on our best face—it's our grown-up room, where we show off our dress-up clothes. That doesn't mean it can't be comfortable or that you can't live in the room. It just means that being at the front of the house (its usual placement) it does command some attention, and sets the tone for the rest of the house.

A few well-chosen pieces—sofa, two chairs, coffee table, lamps—are all you really need to create an inviting atmosphere.

shoes. It's possibly even worthwhile to eliminate a hall closet to give you a spot for sitting down and removing shoes, as long as there's coat storage elsewhere.

Create a focal point—a sculpture on a wall shelf at the far end of a hall, a faux window or mirror.

Mirrors in halls visually enlarge space and bring in more light. A landscape painting that shows a distant horizon also expands space and brings nature indoors—especially effective in a windowless front hall.

Light, neutral walls will expand the hallway space, although this is one area you can afford to be more

My friend Martha is a china collector—her house was filled with beautiful rare pieces, but her living room furniture hadn't been updated or upholstered in years. Then real estate agent Jennifer Bray-Legalle came through with her clipboard, brisk manner and to-do list. Apart from serious decluttering of the china, books and accessories, the wood furniture was painted the same caramel colour, the dining room was restored to its original use (rather than a piano and homework room), the living room sofa was slipcovered and the dark green walls were toned down to a warm wheat colour.

If your living room just doesn't sit right with you, try taking all the furniture out then returning it piece by piece, starting with the largest and most necessary (the sofa). Be careful in your efforts not to leave the room looking like a great void—removing those beautiful Oriental rugs, as patterned as they are, may render the room dull and lifeless. Diane Chaput says vendors often "get" the purging idea a little too well, and she ends up hunting for things they've got stowed to add some life back into their homes.

In a more formal living room, seating will be oriented toward the fireplace (if there is one). In large living rooms, create two or more seating areas—the first around the fireplace, and the others as vignette seating just beyond. Determine where normal walk-throughs are—the routes through to a door, window, chair or another room—and try to avoid placing furniture in the way of these walk-throughs.

If the sofa faces the fireplace and has its back to the entry, position a console table behind and top it with flowers, books, a lamp, and baskets underneath. If you have two loveseats, or a sofa and loveseat, they should face each other perpendicular to the fireplace, with a large round or square coffee table between.

Large mirrors are a great classic—add where possible without overdoing it. People slow down with reflections, but will get freaked out in a house of mirrors. Interesting shapes and different materials all add to the mystique of a passing glimpse—of yourself, the outdoors, a painting.

Fill in empty corners with a vignette—chair and ottoman, a chaise or screen—which draws the eye and expands space.

Be creative with coffee tables. Movable ottomans, four storage cubes grouped, a tall tea table, two tray tables side by side, a trunk or an upholstered bench, all work well for the purpose.

Dining Room

Although the dining room fell out of favour for a long time, it's been steadily regaining ground in popularity. While some houses have the space to accommodate a formal dining room, others incorporate them into the kitchen. Wherever you dine, the aim should be to create a space that emphasizes intimacy and promotes conversation.

Its focus should be the table: does it welcome, are the chairs close together, is the table itself comfortable and not too fussy? Is there a view to capitalize on? Is there a nice centrepiece of flowers or candles?

The basics are table, chairs, storage and display. A table needs to fit within the space and shouldn't either overwhelm or be lost. The chairs should fit comfortably without crowding. Round tables invite conversation and soften a square room. Rectangular tables are traditional and lengthen a short room. Square tables have a more modern feel. Glass tables give sparkle and see-through qualities, but also really show the dust and fingerprints.

Like other rooms, the dining area needs a focal point, and if it's not going to be the table, then consider a breakfront that displays dishes, glasses and art objects, or a buffet with an artful arrangement and a mirror or piece of art on the wall above.

If there's no room for a buffet, consider installing a floating cabinet (a sleek modern wood kitchen cabinet, for example) a few inches above the floor. This will give storage and the space to display things so that the room gets its focal point. Otherwise, you get a forlorn table adrift in the middle of an undefined space.

Where there's only room to install a wide shelf the length of one wall, lean a large mirror, or photographs or prints against the wall and create your focal point that way. Stack baskets under the shelf for extra storage.

In a model suite I saw recently, storage was created in the open concept living and dining room in an ingenious way. The designer, Trevor Kruse, installed three cantilevered shelves, the tallest one about 30 inches off the floor. He painted the walls from the shelving down in the same chocolate brown; above, the wall colour was cream. This gave the appearance of built-in storage, and was great for displaying china and glassware in the dining room, and books and audio-video equipment in the living room.

If your furniture is too big for the space—and in dining rooms this is a common problem—store it and rent something smaller and more streamlined. Then set the table with a nice centrepiece. If your home office is in the dining room, and your desk is a rectangle, consider covering it with a tailored cloth for showings and open houses. If the cloth falls to the floor, you can hide office equipment underneath. Just make sure the tablecloth is in keeping with the overall scheme of your home. Hide bookcases behind a screen or luxurious velvet curtain.

Be creative with centrepieces. A beautiful antique mixing bowl filled with Shasta daisies is a great country look, or bare branches or twigs in tall vases.

In a condo, it's not likely you'll have the space for much of a dining room, but show buyers that entertaining is possible by carving out space in a corner of the living room, or the edge of the hall nearest the kitchen. You can create a dining room with a small table, two to four slim (or folding) chairs, a large mirror, a piece of art and a pendant lamp. Stick with strong shapes and larger accessories (candlesticks, glasses).

A pendant light or chandelier should be no more than 36 inches above the dining table, otherwise it loses connection to the table. The width of the chandelier should be about a foot less than the width of the table. If the chandelier you have seems dated, try slipping a large lampshade over it.

A very formal dining room that is the only space for eating can be toned down a notch or two by exchanging the brass chandelier for a ceiling fan, exchanging the Oriental rug for seagrass, and using bamboo mats and plain dishes instead of fussy china.

If your dining room is used only for evening meals, can the room multitask as a library or a music room without confusing the focus at all? The reality is that many people have a piano in the dining room. But if you're trying to emphasize the room's full potential—dining for both family and guests—then don't confuse the issue, and put the piano in storage.

A settee or loveseat on one side of the dining table reads casual and sophisticated, or try four wooden chairs and two upholstered. If wooden chairs are mismatched, paint them—white, black, baby blue, soft green.

Bedroom

The focal point in this room is, not surprisingly, the bed, so the more luxurious the better. Spend time and money on bed linens as coordinated and sumptuous as possible.

Learn how to make a bed. Four pillows should be propped against the headboard with two accent pillows: Euro shams (larger than average) on two large pillows and two standard shams on smaller. The sheet should be folded down over the blanket, quilt tucked in all around, and duvet or comforter folded at the end of the bed. The way to plump a bed with pillows is to lean two Euro pillows against the headboard, with a smaller square in the middle of those two. For a more minimal look, try one long bolster, or pillows stacked one on top of the other.

A tailored skirt is more updated than ruffled. And if it's a contemporary room, opt for a snug-fitting, quilted material around the boxspring.

You need a headboard. Even if it's just part of a bed propped against the wall behind your bed, it gives definition. Alternatives: a vintage door hung horizontally over the bed, iron grates, fabric draperies the length of the wall, a tapestry or antique kilim, a large antique mirror or picture, a large piece of engraved wood, or a triptych of black-and-white photos in large chunky frames.

The bedspread should drive the colour and style choices of the room. Create a vanity out of a computer desk outfitted with a skirt to

Tomasz Majcherczyk

Left: Buyers expect to see a home office, but when it doubles beautifully as a guest room, all the better. This home office was orange before, with an old sofa, a bookcase, and a desk with computer—Julia and Cesare repainted the room pale yellow, added the guest bed with Pierre Frey linens, some pretty artwork, and voila!

complement the bed linens, and hang a mirror above. Replace overburdened bookshelves with floating shelves.

Make sure the bedding matches—even if it is all white. Model homes often show baths and bedrooms with the boutique hotel look—clean-lined, neutral palettes like French vanilla and shell pink, taupe and pale blue. Buy the best towels and sheets you can—consider them a housewarming gift to yourself for your next house. Classic white always looks fresh.

When the bed is out of direct sight of the door, the bedroom feels more retreat-like. On the other hand, you want to see the focal point as you enter the room, so how you place the bed really depends on the configuration of the room.

Table lamps provide task light for reading, and soften the illumination. A bench at the foot of the bed with a cozy throw anchors the bed as focal point and adds more depth and dimension. You might even consider angling the bed out from the wall to give it greater impact, which will work in a small room, but only if it's not cluttered with any other furniture.

Add as much living space into a bedroom as possible—even a chair and small table invites lounging (then hang a picture beside to balance the grouping). Customize the interior of the

master bedroom closet, with drawers and double rods, etc.

Children's bedrooms are an invitation to go wild with colour and pattern. These rooms are meant for joy and playfulness. Rather than over-theming them, work on creating a vibrant or restful environment for your child. Agent Joy Verde has a hands-off policy when it comes to staging kids' rooms—don't touch them, apart from keeping them scrupulously clean—since it's often too upsetting to the children.

A double headboard against the wall will make a twin bed (positioned sideways) feel like a daybed, and makes a child's room work in a variety of ways when you add bolsters and pillows. A bulletin board will handle the changing artwork displays.

Family Room

A family room doesn't need to be on the first floor. Any room will do—a second-floor bedroom, in the basement, the garage, or an attic. Keep furniture comfortable and colours warm and simple, especially in small or low-ceilinged rooms such as a basement.

Although this is where the family "flops," the room still needs a focal point. Fireplaces aren't the norm in basements but the plug-in types are inexpensive and widely available. Make it an architectural focal point by attaching old, heavy salvaged brackets to the wall and adding either a vintage mantel or a constructed one. If a fireplace is not an option, create another focal point, the obvious one being the TV.

Home Office

Make it look as decorated as the rest of the home, with leather-bound books, framed photos, a great desk lamp, stationery in nice-looking storage, bowls for paper clips and candles and a "catchall" basket on the floor under the desk.

If your home office is not separate but part of another room, try keeping it behind closed doors, in an office armoire, for instance, or find an alternative spot for it, such as a closet or in the basement.

Part of the home office conundrum is what to do with all those files. If you haven't looked at a file or document in a year, except for your personal legal or financial documents, chances are you never will, so start purging. If you're not able to move filing cabinets off-site, at least stow them somewhere out of sight.

One stager told me that she regularly encounters the home office dilemma when she stages a home. Although she tries to find space in the house that can accommodate a home office, she says it also depends on the agent's point of view. Then a Realtor decides a house is more valuable as a three-bedroom, when the current owner has been using it as a two-bedroom plus office, so it's best to follow the Realtor's lead. For example, tucking a writing desk (not so office looking) into a small space, suggests home office, even though you might not have enough space for a formal one.

Laundry Room

All that's expected from the lowly laundry room is something functional and clean, but that doesn't mean it can't be reasonably attractive. Put up a nice shelf, or at least cover the existing one in shelf paper, like crisp faux stainless steel.

Folded towels stacked either on top of the dryer or on a counter have a look of organized cleanliness.

Basement

Avoid thinking of your basement as the repository for all the junk in the rest of the house. Nobody likes clutter, whether it's above or below ground. What you're aiming for is a room that looks like part of the home, something you care about.

Most buyers—especially urban ones—either expect or want extra space in the basement. (It's usually just turned over to the teenagers anyway, but that's the buyer's problem.) This is your opportunity to pull out all the money-saving tricks to make the space look great without going over budget: warm light walls, a plug-in fireplace with low bookshelves on either side, sisal or neutral broadloom for warmth, a comfy sofa and a carefully selected assortment of toys, games and video items to suggest this is the "playroom."

Because basements are usually partially underground, windows tend to be small. So hang full-length curtains all the way to the ceiling and wide of the window to create an illusion of bigger windows. Plantation shutters accomplish the same thing.

Low light levels are a basement's biggest challenge, so pump up the artificial light, either recessed, or enough table and floor lamps to create ambience. If you're lucky enough to have a walkout, reinforce the outdoor connection by framing the glass door with light, pretty curtains, and painting walls a natural earth tone.

Plenty of basements still have wood paneling, a la 1970. Get rid of it, and drywall instead. If you can't, then at least paint the paneling in a light cream or a deeper warm cocooning colour like butter pecan. Consider adding architectural details such as crown moulding and baseboards. As usual, storage is sought after, so add either entertainment armoires or bookcases. (And measure carefully before buying, since not all regular-height bookcases will fit.)

If your basement is open concept, but you want to show dual functions—office space and family room, for instance—use cubby-type bookshelves (like IKEA's "Lack") that divide the areas without cutting the light. It can also serve as organizing centre for both spaces—files with access on one side for the office, and games, DVDs and toys on the other for the family room.

If you have to change the flooring, remember that not all floors work well in below-grade situations like a basement. Hardwood is not a great choice, because even the lowest levels of moisture can cause it to buckle. Both linoleum and Marmoleum, which is a sheet floor made up of mostly natural materials, are great underfoot if it's a kids' playroom. But if the family spends time down there, go for broadloom in a hard, low-pile twist that's cheaper and more durable.

A suspended ceiling is *sooo* last century—those acoustic tiles make a basement look like a basement, so spring for the full drywall ceiling.

Because a basement usually has lower ceilings—unless it's been dug down—open the space with French doors to offices, or bedrooms in the basement.

Match the wall colours to the upstairs as much as possible, or go a few shades lighter to compensate for less natural light. Select furniture that's similar to what you would use upstairs—comfortable but nice looking.

CHAPTER 13
SMALL SPACES *Make the Most of What You've Got*

Being a lousy housekeeper, I've always favoured small spaces—less to clean—but I am also drawn to the creative side of living small, and to the coziness factor. We seem to have a deep-seated need for enclosure, and a small home affords that sense of protection, intimacy and connectedness. But as urban real estate prices skyrocket, small spaces are becoming the only realistic option for many people. Thankfully, buyers are becoming more realistic too.

Still, even the most realistic among us wants to feel that we're buying and moving into a spacious home. To appeal to that desire, you, as a seller, can make use of the two basic ways to maximize a small space: create more *physical* space, usually through efficient built-ins, and/or create more *visual* space.

Physical space

You can create physical space by reducing the number of objects you choose to have. You need seating, storage and lighting, but perhaps not two sofas, one chair, an armoire, a trunk and four floor lamps.

You can also use reduced scale to increase space. A solid-coloured sofa won't intrude into the space, especially if it's a condo size, or is armless or low armed. If you pull up two chairs from the dining table, there's a connection between the spaces that makes for a more cohesive whole.

Rather than having several bookcases or display units dotting the interior landscape, opt for a floor-to-ceiling bookcase to cover one entire wall, or build in bookshelves on either side of a fireplace. An inexpensive alternative is to buy IKEA shelving and have a carpenter finish it to the walls with moulding for a built-in look.

Small dining room, big table? While your house is listed, store your oversized table and chairs and rent a narrow (30-inch) table, with a bench or banquette for one side and two slim parson's chairs for the other. Best to keep dining areas as close

to the kitchen as possible. Many are now turned into home offices, but while the house is listed, it's better to confine the home office to one corner of a room, especially if you have a laptop, and return the dining room to its designated function.

If singles or childless couples are your market, casual eating can be accommodated by an extended counter or breakfast bar with two slim stools tucked up underneath. Alternatively, a wall-mounted table takes little room.

Visual space

There's no end to the visual tricks you can use to make a space feel larger. Here are some.

· Use vertical space—with tall bookcases, shelves or armoires—to draw the eye up.

· For the same reason, hang curtains close to the ceiling. Go for tailored, neatly pleated solid curtains or Roman shades. With curtain panels, make sure the edge hangs beyond the window frame to let as much light in as possible. Natural light opens up a space like nothing else.

· Opt for a varied lighting scheme. In addition to recessed lights (if you have them), add floor and table lamps, and then add a third dimension with wall sconces. Stick with simple, plain solid lampshades.

· If the fireplace is unattractive—red brick and large, for example—use paint, stucco or Venetian plaster in a colour that's the same as or similar to your wall colour to minimize its presence and allow it to recede.

· Choose a single large area rug, rather than several smaller ones. This draws the eye to the perimeter of the room.

· Acrylic or glass coffee tables keep a space light and airy. In the same way, a table with slender legs (as opposed to a trunk or a table with chunky legs) doesn't obstruct light and allows the eye to see through and beyond.

· Mouldings and chair rails are nice, but in a small space cause the eye to jump around. Minimize the visual clutter by painting mouldings and chair rails the same colour as walls. Original details in a home give character, but too many details can diminish the sense of space.

· Reduce the pattern in the room—depth is better added through textured fabrics than with pattern.

· Emphasize negative space (the emptiness around an item) by grouping furnishings in vignettes and leaving free air space around them, choosing furniture with legs instead of skirts, and chairs and sofas with narrow or no arms.

· Fool the eye with large scale. Fewer pieces of larger scale are inviting, and give the feeling of more space to stretch out.

· Monochromatic colour schemes, where all colours are kept close in tone and value, visually expand a room because there is little contrast and the eye can move through a room uninterrupted. To create interest, incorporate a variety of textures within monochromatic

schemes. That doesn't mean you can't paint a room a darker colour for drama and a sense of enclosure (especially effective in a small dining room), but while listing it's probably wiser to opt for smooth transitions between rooms, rather than go for drama. A monochromatic colour scheme (that doesn't necessarily mean beige: it could be blue) makes a house feel as though it goes on forever.

· Light furnishings, ceilings and draperies can open and lighten up a dark room. Light ceilings tend to raise the eye, while dark ceilings tend to lower the eye.

· Unify the walls by painting the trim (baseboards, windows) the same colour; drapery in the same colour as the walls blurs the boundaries between the two elements and helps expand the space.

· Keep window treatments really simple—no deep swags or Kingston valances, but Roman shades and simple lined drapery panels. Where two small rooms open onto one another, repeat window treatments to increase the flow and help enhance a sense of larger space.

· Keep floors one continuous material where possible—tile in the hall, hardwood in the dining room, broadloom in the living room and sheet floor in the kitchen will have your eyes popping all over the place.

· Keep furniture of an appropriate scale to the room—a large chair is fine if the lines are crisp

Below: This small kitchen has plenty of room for a breakfast table and chairs—just keep the furniture to a small scale, and pare back any clutter.

and tailored, but not if it's overstuffed with huge rolled arms and floral upholstery. Keep fabrics on the dark side and not patterned—chairs in light materials appear larger. The reverse holds true for dark stains on wood furniture—so rather than a nice white round wood dining table that will stand out, stain it dark—dark brown for modern looks and matte black for American country, or white for shabby chic looks.

· When furniture contrasts with walls—dark with light—the furnishings appear smaller and the room larger. Upholstering the furniture the same colour as the walls will cause it to disappear, but frankly that's a little safe—and boring.

· Store any furniture with big, busy patterns. Pieces with small patterns—dots or checks, for instance—are fine.

· Mirrors are a small-space friend—they reflect, mimic and create light. If you have two small rooms, one with a window and the other on an interior wall, add a mirror to the inside room so that it can catch the light from the window and bounce it around.

· As always, reduce clutter and pare back the amount of furniture.

· Even though open concept space seems to be the order of the day, it's important to strike a balance between open space and enclosed space. In an open concept space, you don't have to put the walls back up, but consider "enclosing" some areas within the larger space by furniture grouping and room dividing screens. Giving a focus and a function to each part of the space will actually enhance a sense of spaciousness.

Tomasz Majcherczyk

CHAPTER 14
AGENTS, AGENTS EVERYWHERE *How to Make a Choice*

When should you call an agent?

There's a debate among stagers on whether to call the real estate agent before or after you stage your home. A lot of agents suggest calling them first, so they can steer a vendor in the right direction as to what works for the neighbourhood. But Michael Corbett, author of *Find It, Fix It, Flip It!*, advises against calling in an agent until the house is in pristine shape and ready to market, because the agent will carry his or her first impression of the house—no matter how much work is put into it after that first visit.

My advice would be to do the repairs, basic decluttering and cleaning before you call an agent, since you have to do those anyway. And save the styling or switching of rooms until your agent has had a look and can pass judgement.

Does it make a difference which agent you choose?

Designer Nora Lukss answers an emphatic yes to that question. "You bet it does. When we staged our home the first time, we got bad advice from the agent. While he was right about the area demographic and the state of the market, he didn't see the value of working with what the house was, which was a multi-level, very modern structure in the midst of a traditional neighbourhood. He was determined to work against what it was, trying to make it into a traditional family home. That approach just didn't work. Our second agent understood the house and marketed for its features."

When Nora was ready to find a different agent, she created a plan. "I researched agents in our neighbourhood as well as the downtown core of the city, figuring that maybe the buyers would be looking to upgrade from a downtown condo to a house near the lake. I tried to determine the most successful agents in my area, based on the following criteria: the most Sold signs, largest marketing campaigns, most pervasive presence in the community newspapers and personal referrals from satisfied customers."

Nora narrowed her list to four, and interviewed them all in one day. The four represented a diverse range of strategies, personalities, pressure tactics and philosophies. "The last question I asked all of them was: What price would you list this house? The answers were wildly different."

After weighing all the pros and cons of each agent over the weekend, Nora found that one stood out in her mind. "Diane [Chaput] understood the house, the neighbourhood and she believed a certain buyer would ultimately buy this house—and she was right. She's well respected within the real estate community as a person with integrity and I liked her plan."

The agent's fee

As you interview prospective agents, ask about their fees. Historically the seller has been expected to pay a commission of between 5% and 6% of the sale price. This amount is usually split between the seller's agent (sometimes called the listing agent, this is the one working for you, the homeowner) and the buyer's agent, (whoever brings the buyer to the table). The listing and selling agent could be one and the same person, because a real estate agent can represent either the buyer or the seller, or both. In that case, the lower end of the commission scale is the norm.

Either way, the agent must disclose this relationship. Because the agent is supposed to be representing the interests of their client—in this case both buyer and seller—there ends up being a conflict of interest. So it's best to avoid this kind of contract.

But real estate commissions are usually negotiable—in the United States, this is the law, while in Canada, the commission structure varies from Realtor to Realtor. It's advisable to ask any prospective agent about this. For more information on the process, and on the ethical obligations of a real estate agent, visit the website of the Canadian Real Estate Association at www.crea.ca.

Here's what Canadian Mortgage and Housing Corporation (CMHC) has to say about agents and fees: "Your real estate agent's job is to help you find the ideal home, write an Offer of Purchase, negotiate on your behalf to help you get the best possible deal, and provide you with important information about the community, arrange and coordinate the home inspection and essentially save you time, trouble and money." CMHC recommends asking questions when you're interviewing agents—especially about how they charge for their services. As stated above, vendors normally pay a commission to the agent, but some agents charge buyers a flat fee. Use the online guide to what questions to ask your agent: http://www.cmhc-schl.gc.ca/en/co/buho/hostst/wosh_009.cfm?renderforprint=1

Marketing

As you're interviewing agents, you'll want to ask about more than payment structures: you'll also want to know if he or she is a good marketer. How would they word the listing advertisement for your house, for example? While wording might seem like a minor issue, it can have a big effect on home sales. According to a study done by Paul Anglin, a professor of marketing and consumer studies at the University of Guelph, the way you word your listing ad has a huge effect on how quickly and for how much your home will sell. Words such as *granite, beautiful, landscaping, gourmet* and *move-in condition* help move a house faster, while words such as *new paint, as-is, good value, quiet* and *must-sell* translate into longer listings and lower prices.

Every agent has a different marketing approach. While exposure is vital, not all types of exposure are equal. "Good exposure is putting it out for everyone to see on MLS and advertising in the papers," says agent Diane Chaput, "because people still like to browse the weekend paper for real estate."

The jury's out on the value of open houses. Chaput isn't big on them: "Tested sales practice is to tease buyers by not giving them everything. But when you let all these people walk in the door, you've given them everything, and they don't even have their agent there to ask questions. Plus, you've always got someone walking around making critical comments—and usually it's someone browsing but not buying. That can unnerve clients, and I want more control over how someone sees a house."

On the other hand, I have friends who've bought from an open house, although they'd also been browsing MLS for months. Another value of open houses—and agents often hold open houses precisely for this reason—is that you may meet the agent of your dreams, the one who will be the perfect partner for selling your own home, and buying the new one.

What Chaput does is list a house for five or six days on MLS, specifying the day that offers can be made, and ensuring maximum exposure. If an agent sees the listing one day, shows it to clients after lunch, and immediately puts in an offer, that's not enough exposure, since you'll have to deal with that offer before other prospective buyers even get in to see the house. In such cases, says Chaput, "You're always left wondering what if you'd waited a few days for more offers. On the other hand, your first appointments are the most important because they're the ones who've been looking and always asking what's new." In other words, they may be the most motivated and serious buyers currently looking in your area and price range.

Getting the credentials

Ask the agent about their average list-to-sales-price ratio. This tells you what they listed a house for, and what it sold for. If they tend to get close to the listing price, or over, that means they know how to price something to sell. Keep in mind, though, that these list-to-sales-price ratios also reflect how brisk the market is at any given time:

an agent's success rate will be affected—for good or bad—by prevailing trends.

Ask prospective agents for references. Some agents are, to put it bluntly, very difficult to deal with, and with the home sale process as challenging as it can be, why bother with rudeness? Ask references how quick the agent was in responding to their calls, and how patient they were in explaining documentation. And ask your friends and co-workers if they have recommendations for agents they were satisfied with.

Finally, make sure you sign an agreement that you can get out of, should the relationship prove unpleasant or unfruitful. For example, start with a listing agreement for 30 days rather than 60 or 90 days.

A staging relationship

Some agents, like Joy Verde, come with their own staging team as part of the fee structure (major repairs are not included in the package, however). Other agents may suggest a stager, and still others will make suggestions about how to stage it yourself. Chaput falls into the latter category. "I always advise people to keep it fairly simple. Unless it's a major job, I suggest they do it themselves since most people know how to paint the front door. I used to suggest a paint colour for the house or the front door, but invariably people would say no, I don't like that colour. So now I say: You think of a colour. They take it on,

and I always come back in a week to a totally transformed home."

But when Chaput tells clients they have only a week to fix their home, they blanch and look "panic stricken," until she explains that the one-week mark is when photos will be taken. During that time, they can store things in the basement, while figuring out where to store them for the open house and showings. "Once things are in the basement," Chaput says, "people usually find they don't need half the stuff and get rid of it."

Where Chaput draws the line at staging is with estate sales. "You have elderly people or a family grieving; it's too much to put them through the fluffing exercise. It's cruel to say that this needs help or they should rip up the carpet—these things are major to them. In those situations, I might help with clutter, and suggest keeping out some wonderful pieces and putting the rest away. But you don't try to make it taupe and granite."

Pricing

Although proper staging should positively affect the price, one stager said to me, "I'm not a miracle worker. If your house isn't priced right, it doesn't matter what I do to it, it won't sell."

So, how do agents come up with the right listing price for your house? They look at all the other properties in the neighbourhood, and compare apples with apples—or at least they should. If you're wondering why your three-bedroom semi isn't listed the same as the three-bedroom semi up the street, there may be a number of factors:

· the level of repairs done
· the level of perks—new kitchen, baths, flooring, etc.
· the level of staging
· the location on the street—are you next to a gas station, cemetery, hydro pole or the busy intersection?
· the lot size and dimensions. Agents have told me that a lot of 140-feet deep is more desirable than a lot only 100-feet deep, but that anything deeper than 140-feet is a waste. Is it a narrow yard? Is there parking?

Agents also have different strategies. Some prefer to list low so they can start a bidding war. Others prefer to list right on target, fearful that there will be only one buyer, who will come in low. Still others prefer to list high, in hopes of enticing vendors to list with them.

Chaput, the agent who listed Nora's house successfully, says no matter how much staging you do, the stars have to align in other areas, too. "Everything has to feel right—if the interior looks good, but the price isn't right, you'll hear little complaints, because buyers feel it's listed too high and they're looking for certain things. But if all the elements are right—a great interior, a good price—you don't hear the complaints."

While it's tempting to go with the agent who gives you the highest selling price, that can be a fatal trap. In an earlier chapter, I mentioned a house up the street from me that was priced about $100K too high. Once it got stale, which only takes a few short weeks, everybody steered clear of it. Even in a fairly brisk market, it sat for over a year.

If your agent lists high and your house languishes on the market for months—as the house up the street did—you've gained nothing and lost a lot. If the sellers up the street had done their research, they might have found out that the agent has a reputation for listing too high. They could have steered clear of that situation.

Another factor that affects price is the vagaries of the market. When the market is on its way up or down, prices can be volatile (that is, one week they can be higher than the next), and they tend to do a zigzag motion all over the pricing map. It's very hard to pinpoint what the price should be within that given two weeks. For example, a semi-detached house up the street from me was listed at $349K about a year ago. The two detached houses beside it were also listed. One sold but the other sat there, as did the semi. Fast-forward nine months, and the semi went up for sale for $389K in a market that was supposedly going soft, and sold over asking in a couple of days. Go figure…

BUYER'S MARKET—SELLER'S MARKET

In a buyer's market, there are more homes available to buy than people who want to buy. With more inventory, houses tend to sit longer because buyers can take their time to browse and can expect more out of a house. And they can be extremely picky. In this kind of market, how you show your home is very important—hence the value of home staging.

In a seller's market, there are fewer houses than buyers, who then don't have the luxury of taking time to make a decision. Homes sell fast, and often with multiple offers. Home staging is a benefit even in this kind of market, since in a seller's market everyone is trotting out anything they can get their hands on—even the dog's breakfast. So a good-looking house can raise prices even higher.

The agents' open house: what to expect

The agents' open house is an opportunity for other agents to see your property. Since agents usually have buyers they're working with, this is a chance for them to really see what the property has to offer and determine if it might work for their clients. But it's normally the case that agents don't make comments one way or the other about the house, the staging or the price—at least not to the listing agent.

What to do before every showing

· Air out house for half an hour, opening windows and doors.
· All areas: dust and touch up floors with vacuum.
· Kitchen: stove, oven, sink spotless; counters clear and clean; floors cleaned.
· Bathrooms: fresh towels, counters clear and clean, sink and faucet spotless.
· Bedrooms: no clutter, kids' toys staged, beds made properly. (Diane Chaput regularly arrives a half-hour before her agent open house to make the beds. Most people pull the cover to the top of the bed and leave it at that, so she tucks the sheets in nice and tight, and draws the bedspread or duvet back, then adds more pillows. The room is transformed.)
· Twice a day while your house is listed, do a walk-around with a basket for picking up items and returning them to their rightful place.
· Turn on all lights, make sure temperature is comfortable, and turn on fireplace during cold weather.
· Check that flowers are fresh.
· Set music to play. Make sure it's got universal appeal, and widely recognized, like Vivaldi's

Four Seasons—no heavy metal, rap or strange jazz pieces (although some blues and jazz are quiet and soothing).
· Outside: lawn cut, leaves raked, garden tools stowed away, trash cans out of sight.
· Set up a laptop presentation of the house as it's used.
· Display before and after photos of major remodelling projects.

Smells

· The best smell is cleanliness and should come from natural, everyday things—baking bread, herbs drying in the window, fresh laundry, etc.
· Avoid heavy cooking smells the night before showings.
· Try to arrange for a kennel to take your pets while the house is listed—you may not notice the odour, but others will. At the very least, take them out of the house during the open house, and subsequent showings. If they must remain in the house, for whatever reason, at least put them in a carrier, with a note not to touch.
· Smell is subconscious and draws us as much as sight or the other senses, but many people have allergies to perfumes, so don't go overboard with potpourri.

PART 2 *Case Studies*

STRETCHING SPACE
Design consultant Jennifer Brouwer creates beauty and efficiency in a tiny condo

Housing Type
Small condo (about 670 square feet), in a desirable area of downtown Toronto.

Selling History
This condo was purchased for about $179K, three years ago, as university housing for the owner's daughter and her roommate. After her daughter's graduation, the owner's initial intent, because of the loft's proximity to the financial district, was to refurbish it for executive rentals, especially for executives on contract living temporarily in the city. But she changed her mind and decided to sell. The condo sold in a matter of days for $300K.

Stager
Jennifer Brouwer is an interior design consultant and owner of décor by Jennifer Inc. As a full-service design consultation company, most of their business is residential, but she is finding more recently that clients really want help in staging their homes for sale.

Features
Although the condo was small, it had high ceilings and an efficient layout.

Deficiency List
· Concrete floors, walls and ceiling were not conducive to traditional elegance or the executive luxury that the area would demand.
· Bedroom measured only 10 feet by 10 feet.
· Biggest issue was light, since there was only one large window, and that window's style was challenging to hang drapes on.
· The furniture was a hodgepodge of futons, desks, computers and lots of bedding.

What Jenn Did

Jenn says that though you could do this condo over in a couple of weeks, she gave herself six weeks to allow for custom-made draperies and bedding. It was important to gear the look of the condo to the demographic likely to buy (or rent, as they'd initially expected) in the area.

"These weren't exactly the tidiest university kids—and they didn't have much furniture," Jennifer recalls, so there was a fair bit of fixing, customizing and furniture placement to do.

Because of certain constraints—particularly the industrial feel of the concrete floors and walls—Jenn felt it important to continue with the industrial loft sensibility, but to dress it up in a glamorous, retro way. Hence the golden palette, luxurious materials, sparkling vintage mirrors and early 20th-century antiques (secretary desk and filing cabinet).

The first thing Jennifer addressed was the lack of light, so she brought in an electrician, who ran electrical boxes on the ceiling to accommodate the extra lighting—large, beautiful modern lights. Recessed (pot) lights weren't possible without dropping the ceiling, so Jenn says she went with a "feminized" industrial look instead.

Next, she patched areas of the concrete walls, though no drywall was installed. The walls were then painted—an accent wall in Adam's Gold and the others in a greyed-out green called Herbes de Provence (both from Benjamin Moore), which was also used in the faux glazing treatment on the porous concrete floor.

The earthy golden colour palette was soothing and kept the space open while providing lots of depth, Jenn explains.

The oddly shaped window needed to be worked around, too. Because of the ductwork, Jenn had to custom order a Roman blind to fit exactly around the perimeter, without drawing attention to the shape. Vertical stripes on silk fabric Romans minimized the shape in the best way possible.

When it came to furniture layout, Jenn had to first declutter and remove all the university-style furniture and accessories, and then make over the condo into a sensational multi-functional small space. The living room got a sofabed, two comfortable, smaller-scale black leather club chairs and a "coffee table" from a pair of cube ottomans.

Rohan Laylor

Two focal points created some interest in the living area: a wall of exquisitely framed mirrors hanging behind the sofabed and an antique secretary desk on the opposite wall. "It was such a large wall, and the grouping of pretty mirrors worked well to open the space while incorporating light and sparkle," Jenn says.

Certain accessories, like the antique Fitz and Bowes secretary, and the dental cabinet in the bedroom, made sense in the industrial context. And funky graphic fabric stretched over canvas enhanced the retro feel she was going for.

A simple sisal carpet pulled the elements together while adding a natural element. Nesting tables tucked beside the sofa, and a small round bar server table, expand for entertaining.

A symmetrical design approach—which included painting one wall darker to balance the height of the secretary on the other wall—maximized the space in the living room.

The dining area, incorporated into the kitchen, comprised a round maple table, bistro style, with two small chairs. What defined the space as a special dining spot was a focal point installation piece of nine mini-mirrors.

In the bedroom, Jennifer's aim was to soften the industrial look with silk bed covers, a drum light, a pretty mirrored end table and a large floor mirror. And to max out closet space, Jennifer hired an organizer company to create a full eight feet of storage from the closet.

As a final touch, faux plants were brought in. As Jennifer says, it adds life, and every place needs a bit of green. "I don't agree with agents who say plants have to be real—that's nonsense—these are versatile, low maintenance and inexpensive. When buyers traipse through your home, they're not analyzing the brand, but soaking up the ambience to see if it suits them."

Jenn's Tips

· My number-one philosophy is to have fun, and create a feeling or mood.

· A buyer should never feel the need to focus on one item, but should be in awe of the space in its entirety.

· The style or period don't matter. It's important to figure out the big picture by starting in the foyer and going through the rooms, asking, What do you like about this area, what do you want to change, what do you want to keep?

· If you love something, work with it, but if you don't, toss it.

· A home has to be priced right—we aren't miracle workers.

· You need to put in money to make money, but you also need to draw the line on staging; how much you spend depends on what you paid, whether you can do some of the work yourself, and what is the top price your neighbourhood can sustain. Answering these questions will tell

Photos by Rohan Laylor

Below: A path of small round area carpets leads the way through the entry into the condo. Jenn keeps things symmetrical with a console table and two slim pictures above.

you how much you stand to gain.

· Sometimes it's better not to buy furniture. If rental is priced right, and can help you create a gorgeous space, then rent—it's better to have a few glamour items than a bunch of junk.

· People's first instinct is to shop when they decide to sell, but it's better to carefully select from among the items you already have, which will help emphasize the space because that's what you're selling.

· It all comes down to scale—buyers don't care about the cost of a sofa; it's the scale of it that matters. "I've gone into condos with puffy couches—yes, they're comfy and durable, but they don't belong in a condo because they're way too big."

· Best to have a one-year plan when contemplating selling because in some homes there are repairs to do and it's hard to hurry those things along.

· Clear the slate, pick out what you have that you love and will show off the room, and then put the rest back (toss or store).

· Accent colours can pull several areas together, especially when a home is open concept. For example, an accent colour on the fireplace wall can be brought into the seats of the dining room.

Rohan Laylor

Below: A small bistro table and two chairs create a breakfast nook and can be pulled out when company comes. Mirror tiles over the table set the vignette apart from the working aspect of the kitchen.

Rohan Laylor

FROM FUNKY BOHO TO PEACEFUL RETREAT

Designer Paula Whitlock creates ideal out of idiosyncratic

Housing Type

Moderately priced, semi-detached brick home in a family-oriented neighbourhood.

Selling History

This was the home's first time for sale since the owners bought it 14 years ago. They had gradually done work on the home, such as gutting and renovating the kitchen, and massively overhauling the garden. The house listed in the high 300s, and sold for about $50K more than the asking price, setting a precedent for the street.

Stager

Paula Whitlock graduated from interior design in 2003, and has found that a good portion of her business is in staging. She and Lynn, one of the homeowners, have been good friends for many years.

Features

The house had a huge, recently renovated kitchen, and beautiful gardens front and back.

Deficiency List

· Only one second-floor bathroom, which was tiny and had never had work done. (And one bathroom in the basement.)
· Colours too strong.
· Artistic family with lots of books, art and nice things, but it was too much.

What Paula Did

Paula and Lynn, the homeowner, are good friends. Once Lynn and her partner, Wayne, had decided they were selling, she gave up her "emotional attachment" to the house and started to prepare with a good decluttering. Fourteen years of work,

Below: The previous putty walls were too muddy and dark for the strong red of the vintage sectional sofa—pale cream is just the right tone to highlight rather than compete with it. Polka dot pillows, sewn by Paula, and a modern graphic rug, allow for some textural interest and visual movement in the room.

travel and living had resulted in accumulated memories, tons of books and unusual art.

She says the decluttering was a real eye-opener. "It's a psychological thing, especially for kids who have to be in on it." It's so huge and so demanding that she advises anyone who's even thinking about moving to plan ahead.

Lynn learned the hard way. She had originally called Paula in just for a colour consult, but ended up doing every single room in the house. It took eight people—Paula, Lynn and Wayne and their nephew, plus a crew of four hired help—three solid weeks to do further decluttering, repairs, painting and staging.

"It was way more than I thought, and it always is, apparently," says Lynn. "We worked non-stop for about three weeks, and practically killed ourselves. It's one thing to paint; it's another to do plaster."

Paula, who tacked up a big Bristol board task sheet in the kitchen, adds: "You really have to stay focused and very organized, assigning people to do one job at a time."

To Lynn's declutter efforts, Paula added her own. "I took half the furniture out, and put most of the books, artwork, record albums, etc., into storage. We set aside the items and art that we thought we would re-use. They'd collected a number of very

interesting things on their travels, like African art. But my feeling is it shouldn't be quite that personal. Leave a few choice pieces, but mostly pare back, pare way back."

As the project evolved, they edited out more large pieces of furniture: a desk, a clothing wardrobe and other beat-up furniture. "I know I was erring on the side of a look that was clean and uncluttered," Paula says. "People who are coming to view the property want to envision themselves in the house, and not feel like intruders by viewing too many personal items."

Lynn remembers her knee-jerk reaction to this editing. "The majority of my favourite stuff was put

away, and the stuff that was brought in was tamer. That's where I as a homeowner had to have a stern talk with myself and not take it personally."

With the decluttering done, the repairs could be tackled. Although a lot of fixing had already been done a few years before—the renovated kitchen was huge and beautiful, the basement was comfortable, the main floor hardwood had been replaced and wide plank pine subfloors upstairs had been sanded and polyurethaned—some things were still outstanding.

The master bedroom had new windows, but two cracks on the interior wall had to be repaired. The walls were then painted buttercream, and the

honey-coloured wooden bifold closet doors were painted out in creamy white.

The third bedroom, being used as a home office, was turned back into a bedroom. Minor drywall holes were patched, and the walls painted a fresh pale yellow, a white roll-up blind was installed over the closet where doors had been removed, and white gauzy curtains were hung in the window.

The two bathrooms needed the most work. Upstairs, a tiny 5-foot by 8-foot space couldn't be altered at this late date, but it could be repaired. Plaster was replaced, new lighting installed, the claw foot tub got a new shower ring and fixture, walls got a fresh coat of white paint and a new medicine cabinet was hung over the sink.

The basement bathroom, which had a shower, needed paint, new shelving and toilet holder, and there were chipped tiles that had to be replaced.

One glass door in the shower was broken and couldn't be replaced in time, since it was special order, so they disclosed that the door was broken and used a shower curtain.

What the main floor and basement needed most was paint. The living room was a dark putty colour, but, given the bright red sectional and the vibrant modern floral carpet, Paula felt that a lighter shade would work better for balance. Half the furniture in the house had been removed, but she was hunting for the right chair to lend balance to the large red sectional. When shopping failed her, she turned to neighbours, from whom she got a handsome black leather tufted club chair.

The basement, recently renovated, was highly functional as a teen hangout, with a dark green oversized sectional and large, wooden entertainment unit. The carpet, though, needed replacing, so she went with a wheat-colour Berber. The walls were white, but Paula felt they needed brightening so they got a coat of warm barley yellow. This colour was carried through to the extra bedroom, whose previous incarnation had been a teenager's bedroom with blood-red walls and ceiling, and a compilation of mismatched, tatty furniture.

"We painted the whole house various shades of neutrals," Paula says. "The kitchen was supposed to also have a new paint job, but after lightening up the living room, we could see that the warm brown tones worked extremely well—it was warm and comforting, and the cupboards stood out. So all we did was refresh two walls with the same colour."

Paula, who's an inveterate shopper, picked up new linens for all the beds—and also found a wicker headboard at IKEA for $15. "I'm a good shopper because I'm out there all the time and know where things are. IKEA is a good place for freshening up, along with HomeSense, and Winners. And Loblaws Superstore is surprisingly good: you can get nice shower curtains, and glassware, and recently I saw they had some floor vases for about $40—a real deal."

She brought artwork from her own house—and where she had none, she created it. Upstairs, a gallery wall was wrought from the plain hall by framing black-and-white photographs that were photocopied from a book. In the main entrance,

three large pieces of art were easily crafted out of photocopies of old Persian carpets, which were then mounted on small foam pieces and framed to resemble a shadow box. When Paula added her signature and a number in the bottom corner, they looked like originals.

Paula also sewed most of the cushions and some of the drapes. Since there wasn't a headboard in the master bedroom, and Lynn didn't want to buy one, Paula chose complementary fabric and sewed covers for two 28-inch by 28-inch pillows—"a nice solution that gave the bed more presence."

Filmy sheers from IKEA were hung on thin rods and then cut to length, and paired with drapes repurposed from the living room, but originally off the rack from Zellers—"right colour, wrong room," Paula says.

The collaboration of Lynn's irrepressible personality and Paula's careful paring back worked phenomenally well. What might have ended up, in different hands, as either overwhelming or totally drab turned out to be a warm, colourful and welcoming home. Lynn was really happy working with Paula. "In such a stressful time, she was such a pleasure," says Lynn, "able to handle all the work, but she was cheerful too.

Paula's Tips

· Clutter becomes a massive task if you don't stay on top of it.

Below: The basement had all the elements necessary for a family room—all it needed was new wheat coloured berber carpeting and walls changed from white to pale yellow. The red ottoman adds some punch, drawing the eye to the centre of the room, and visually expanding the borders.

· Make sure wall colours interchange. You don't want to break up the rooms with different colours. Colour repetition is important—make sure there are hits throughout the house.

· If you need new furniture, rent it, don't buy—you don't know what you'll need down the road.

· I could have gone to town with the other two bedrooms, but didn't have the time. If you want to stage a bedroom and don't have enough of the materials on hand, or the time, aim for fresh and simple. It's the easiest look to digest.

· What people are looking for in a house these days depends on who's looking. A family looks for enough bedroom space, an eat-in kitchen or a family room. A single person may want more contemporary, for entertaining; families don't entertain as much. Lynn designed this kitchen as the heart of the house, for a family but for entertaining as well.

· You want to make the rooms look as spacious as possible without looking stark. Square footage, or the perception of it, makes the buyer feel like they are getting good value for their money.

Colours (all Benjamin Moore)

Living room: CC-280 almond bisque
Basement rooms: CC-180 barley
Upstairs bathroom: CC-40 cloud white
Staircase hallway: CC-280 almond bisque
Master bedroom: CC-260 buttercream
Rear bedroom and middle bedroom: HC-4 Hawthorne yellow
Front door: CC-64 Bonaparte red
All trim: CC-40 cloud white
Kitchen: HC-86 Kingsport gray

HAPPILY WE PURGE

Stager Shona Fitzgerald purges 12 years of a bachelor's life

Housing Type

Large suburban home, north of Toronto.

Selling History

This home was the residence of a very busy dentist who spent most of his time at work. He purchased it 12 years ago and did almost no repairs or updating over the time he had it. Apart from repairs, the entire staging job cost roughly $10K for three months of work. It was listed for around $520K and sold in a few days for $518K.

Stager

Although Shona Fitzgerald started off in footwear, her passion has always been houses. She has been staging her own homes for sale since 1988. She now works in partnership with Jennifer Brouwer at décor by Jennifer Inc.

Features

This relatively new home was solidly built, on a ravine lot. It was large and spacious, and the big windows made it bright and sunny.

Deficiency List

· Very cluttered, it felt more like a way station than a home.
· Kitchen and baths were very dated.
· Whole house needed new lighting.
· Every window needed treatments.
· Brick fireplace in family room was dated.
· No consistent colour scheme.
· No furniture to speak of.

What Shona Did

After taking away three Dumpster loads of stuff—including old sheets, old clothes, 12 years of filing for the owner's office, carpeting, window coverings and chairs from the 1980s—Shona was able to assess the structural needs.

Although the roof, plumbing and wiring were fine, other basic repairs needed doing. Though mostly cosmetic—refacing the kitchen cabinets and the family room fireplace, replacing tile floors with hardwood, replacing kitchen counters and painting the whole house—they added up cost-wise.

Shona opted not to redo the two bathrooms even though they were dated. "It was just too major an undertaking, the elements were in good shape, and a change of wall colour and accessories showed the rooms in their best light," she reasoned. Holdovers from the late 1980s, one bath was pink-hued, while the other was grey, including the toilet and tub. Changing the fixtures would have been very expensive, so she toned them down by painting the walls in Muslin (Benjamin Moore). New light fixtures were added, cabinets were painted a fresh white and the big mirrors were trimmed with new frames.

The kitchen required the most structural work, although even that was mostly cosmetic: replacing the tile floor with hardwood, refacing cabinets with cream recessed panel doors, counters done in granite-look laminate, and new lighting—a pretty chandelier over the island, and a glass pendant over the breakfast table.

The refacing cost about $4,000, which Shona says made good economic sense since the basic cupboards were sound and refacing was faster and cheaper than replacing. Walls were painted Waterbury cream, and a new striped valance freshened the whole space and showed off the wonderful view. A new deck off the kitchen doors, sprayed with an opaque stain and furnished with table and chairs, became a perfect outdoor spot to entertain.

The rest of the house required only cosmetic changes. Fresh paint was used throughout. Even the inside of the front door was painted the same colour as walls and wainscoting for a more finished look.

Once the structural repairs were completed throughout the house, Shona took three days to style, including one full day for hanging window treatments. She added an upholstered bench with brown silk pillows, wall sconces and a tall topiary tree to create a warm welcome in the foyer.

Immediately next to the entry is the living room, accessible through double French doors. She transformed it from a storeroom for office file overflow to a welcoming space with warm tawny-gold walls, silk panel drapery, a red sofa, two William Morris side chairs, an Oriental rug and an oversized ottoman/coffee table.

Rohan Laylor

Between this living room and the kitchen and family room was a small dining room. Its dramatic makeover included walls awash in a deep red, to contrast with the pale bleached-oak dining table, chairs and buffet. A large ebony mirror over the buffet reflects the sparkle of the crystal chandelier, and adds that vital touch of black to ground any space. Custom Roman blinds lend a touch of pattern, while silk drapery panels are rich and luxurious.

In the family room, the former ugly red brick fireplace was refaced with an architecturally detailed white wood mantel, making this room both comfortable and elegant.

Although Shona needed a substantial number of accessories—topiaries, large mantel mirror, several table lamps—what really gave the room warmth and filled it in were custom window treatments. She says custom drapery is worth the expense, even for staging. "You can buy ready-made panels, but they don't have quite the heft and feel of quality that custom does with its nice pleats and lining," she explains. To keep within budget, though, she

shopped at an outlet store, choosing a poly-silk for the panels, and splurging on higher-priced fabrics for Roman blinds, which require less fabric.

Upstairs, the bedrooms were all painted warm, creamy colours, and then furnished from the truckloads of pieces that Shona rented: headboards, night tables, dressers, floor mirrors, side chairs, lamps and candles.

Lighting was an important addition to this staging project. Homes built 20 years ago, Shona says, didn't consider interior lighting schemes the way they do now. "It's fairly typical to find a 20-year-old subdivision house with only one light—that's only 120 watts—per space, so we had to pump up the ambient and task light, and add mirrors to reflect light and add sparkle."

Shona's Tips

· Shopping for a house is the same as fashion: don't buy separates, buy an outfit. In a house, buy shams, cover, skirt—the whole bedroom—at once.

· Figure out your main components—their function, how much you require, how much

Rohan Laylor

the space will allow—then layer in the colour components, soft accessories and cushions. Next, add ambient and task lighting, and anything to make each room bigger and brighter, such as mirrors and other reflective surfaces, and finally bring in the life—plants and art.

· Consider circulation and flow; three things help to achieve this—lighting, paint coordinates and consistent style of furnishings. A major problem is "theme rooms," where each room has its own theme or style. You may like all of those looks, but if there's no way to bring them together and connect them, it will look strange.

· At the end of the day everyone has a budget. Although this home—untouched for 12 years— needed a larger budget, there's quite a bit you can do for $2,000. A gallon of paint only costs $50, and you can paint, freshen, clean, edit and pare back; improve the lighting, buy fresh throws for sofas, pay for a three-hour designer consultation, which will provide a fairly defined list, and buy fresh bedding and towels.

· If it's an empty house, go heavier on furniture and lighter on accessories, because renting accessories is way more expensive than furniture

in proportion to what they contribute to the overall look.

· There are three levels of staging: the rock bottom is a fluff, where you edit and style the space. The length of time taken depends on how much has to be decluttered—if you're a clutter bug and don't part with things well, it's going to take you a while. The next level would be painting, adding area rugs and styling. The last level is a whole-house redo, with rental furniture—typical for large empty homes.

· People's first instinct is to shop when they decide their home needs a change, but that's backwards. You need to clear out things first, develop a floor plan, reposition your own things to fulfil the space plans, and only shop to fill gaps. In most homes, the stuff is already there. In homes where it isn't, rentals are the way to go.

Colours (all Benjamin Moore)

Main floor: Delaware putty for the main colour, and buttercream the secondary
Foyer: enoki
Kitchen: HC-31 Waterbury cream
Dining room: CC-62 sundried tomato
Upstairs hall: haybale
Bathroom cabinets: 2148-60 timid white
Bathroom: CC-110 muslin
Master bedroom: CC-120 stonehouse
Even the inside of the front door was painted

the same as the walls and wainscoting. "Painting the interior door looks more finished," Jennifer says. "It blends with the house, and doesn't stand out like a white door does. An entrance has to look warm and inviting, especially when you have a grand foyer like this one."

Rohan Laylor

Below: The master bedroom looks enormous now with a beautifully dressed bed, low level lighting and mirrored night tables.

Rohan Laylor

TWEAKING THE LAYOUT
Designer Allison Roberts makes small adjustments for maximum yield

Housing Type

Small two-bedroom condo in an industrial area of Toronto

Selling History

This condo was originally listed in the spring and fall of 2006 at $214,900, but yielded little buyer interest. It was then listed in January 2007 at $224,900 after the owners invested $1,200 in staging. The home sold for $224K in two days.

Stager

Allison Roberts is a registered interior design consultant whose business is roughly divided between staging homes for sale and designing homes to stay. Her company is called Burloak Home Staging & Design, and her website is: www.burloakhomestaging.ca.

Features

This spotlessly clean, two-bedroom condo has large windows and a nice layout. The owners' staging was already so pared back, that the home was easy to work with.

Deficiencies

The condo was located in an industrial area of Toronto's west end, and the view from the living room windows was less than attractive. It was also small, around 700 square feet, compounded by large-scale furniture that was pushed to the perimeter of the rooms. The furniture oriented the focus to the window and its less than perfect view—in other words, attracting all the attention to the deficiencies the sellers needed to minimize, rather than highlighting the features of the space.

Allison Roberts

The homeowners' adventures in colour led them down the wrong paths—teal green in the second bedroom, red in the kitchen, icy green-blue in the bathroom and vibrant blue in the master bedroom. "In and of themselves, the colours weren't bad—people are taught to go dramatic," says Allison, "and having red in a kitchen or dining room is great. The problem is those colours didn't work with the components of these particular rooms."

For one thing, the dining area was too small to allow for red walls. And in order to have restful bedrooms, more subdued colours are needed. The other thing about such bright colours is that not everyone likes them, and you are trying to appeal to a mass audience when you're selling your home, Allison explains.

Furnishings were overscaled for the rooms: a loveseat on one wall of the living room and a sofa on the other—perimeter décor, is what Allison calls it. Opposite each other, these large pieces created a bowling alley that "led your eye right to the window," exaggerated by a dining room table that ran the length of the space.

Lastly, the accessories were too small to make an impact: small lamps and picture frames, wicker baskets that impeded access to kitchen cabinets and only succeeded in creating clutter.

What Allison Did

Because the condo was already fairly tidy, Allison didn't have much cleaning and purging to do, except for the odd bit of clutter. In the bathroom, she replaced a white storage cabinet with a simple wicker basket of rolled white towels.

Allison's first step was to paint everything but the open concept living and dining room. The

Left: Keep it simple for maximum effect. With the bed positioned in the centre of the room, the matching night tables (round MDF tables with cloth skirts), glass lamps and accessories, the room has a pleasing symmetry.

Below: The loveseat was removed from the living room and placed in the second bedroom, which functioned as a home office and guest bedroom.

bedrooms she painted a light almond, a fresh neutral that worked well with the wood bed frame, the floral art, red pillow sham, brown-skirted end tables and glass lamps. The bathroom and red kitchen were transformed with a butter pecan colour that complemented the caramel tiling in both spaces and the honey oak cabinets, as well as the white appliances in the kitchen.

To correct the furniture layout problem, Allison removed the loveseat from the living room and placed it in the second bedroom (now a den and home office). Without the loveseat, there was room to bring in the wingback chair, which she placed in front of the window.

While it didn't obstruct the view, the chair did foreshorten the perception of the space and stopped the eye short of the view out over the railway lands. It also created a conversational grouping with the sofa—subtle but effective. Allison chose not to add a coffee table or ottoman because she wanted to create more space and show that you could fit in a full-size sofa.

She pulled the furniture away from the walls without obstructing traffic patterns, including the dining table that had been pushed against the wall. The dining hutch was moved to the wall where the loveseat had been. The hutch's bulk partially concealed the TV that was centred on the wall beside it, and opposite the couch.

With matching end tables and glass lamps on either side of the sofa, the living space had a pleasing symmetry, serving to pull the eye away from the window and the view. The lamps added necessary task lighting for extra warmth and light.

And lastly, she created lifestyle—it wasn't a family building, and she deliberated over whether to bring in a bed for the second bedroom, or keep it as an office. Since the building is geared to professionals, and younger couples, she decided to show a loveseat for guest sleeping, and a home office, with Paris-themed stationery and accessories.

A throw over the chair was a cozy touch, and dressed it up a bit.

Allison's Tips

· Consider demographics—where you have young professionals who like to entertain and have no kids, that second bedroom makes a nice home office and guest room.

Allison Roberts

Allison Roberts

Left: Allison's approach is always simplicity. Cream walls were a much better choice than mint green; the tiles show up better and it's calmer. A simple basket holds towels and fills the white gap between tub and toilet.

· Take rooms back to where they're meant to be, with accessories that telegraph the function.
· If you can't create the wow factor with your own things, then rent or buy a few key pieces—basically don't do half a job, do the whole thing or it just won't work.
· Rent furniture that fits with the home—if it's a high-end home, it needs high-end furnishings; you're selling a lifestyle to a particular target market.
· Hunt for things on sale, like the Nate Berkus living room lamps (half price from Linens 'n Things at $60 apiece).
· Do what makes sense for the budget—for example, there were verticals on the windows, and the homeowners were considering drapes, but I said don't. The sun is strong, and window treatments are necessary to filter light; the only successful thing would have been a custom-made drape, which was prohibitively expensive just for staging, so we kept the verticals, and pulled

them right back.
· Add lamps for more light—they give a warm glow even on the sunniest day, so that buyers can look at the details of the space; millwork, fireplace and other architectural features.
· When it comes to accessories, you want people to slow down and enjoy, but not so much they get distracted.
· Pare back your display items—if there's too much, you can't see the beautiful forest for the clutter of trees, so pick key items to show off, and remove the rest.
· In a nutshell, do whatever it takes to highlight key features and architectural elements. Showcase what the bare bones of space has to offer.

Colours (all Benjamin Moore)
Bedrooms: CC-110 muslin
Kitchen and bathrooms: 2165-70 butter pecan

BEAUTY REVEALED
How stager Bruno Billio subtly pares back layers

Housing Type

Large detached brick home in a high-end north Toronto enclave.

Selling History

This family—two working parents and young twin boys—felt they needed more space, but loved the neighbourhood, so they purchased a larger home up the street. The staging took a little less than two days, and the house went on the market at $779K, and sold in eight days for $70K over asking.

Stager

Bruno Billio is more than just one of the few male home staging experts I know—he's also a talented sculptor and installation artist of common objects like tables, chairs, books and suitcases, which he stacks and balances. With his background in fine arts, and his innate sense of caprice, Bruno is a welcome addition to home staging, though he prefers to call himself a house jockey. Why? Because he can jockey a house into first place in the race to sell.

Features

This gorgeous house is in close proximity to the downtown core and has large gracious principal rooms. It's got three bathrooms, recently sanded and stained hardwood floors, and lots of nice architectural details, like wide trim, door mouldings, and high baseboards. The many windows bring in natural light, and the generous bedrooms are a real selling feature.

Deficiency List

· There was clutter, but most of it was toys everywhere.

- The basement felt more like a "wreck" room—old, dated, uninviting.
- Carpets covered a big selling feature—the hardwood floors!
- Mismatched everything in the master bedroom.
- Paint needed some touch-ups especially on the trim which had been nicked at child height—about two feet from the ground.

What Bruno Did

Like most young families, the twin boys in this home "ran the roost when it came to toys and things," Bruno recalls. So he sat down with the parents and children to discuss what needed to be done. There was some serious decluttering, especially of toys, which had to happen. But it had to be broached with care, since staging—and selling your home—isn't just a physical exercise but an emotional one as well, Bruno finds. "It's not just about staging for now, but a learning process of letting go of some old ideas, and grasping onto new ones, which they'd then be able to take to their new home."

His aim was to make the house look larger, brighter, reveal all its best details and to demonstrate how well rooms function and relate to each other.

First came the decluttering, especially with the toys—removing them altogether from the living room, corralling them into storage in the boys' bedroom, and turning the drab basement into a usable family room, where playing and toys would be a more appropriate feature.

The lovely formal dining room also needed some cleaning. Only occasionally used for family dinners or entertaining, it had become the family drop-off centre, and the table was piled high with books, projects and mail.

Photographs had to be sorted through, as well. It's okay to have some family photographs, especially if they're nice compositions—mom and baby on a beach, for example. But Bruno draws the line at classroom or graduation pictures. "Treat family photos like a piece of art, but they shouldn't command a room. Clear small side tables of all those frames so the space can breathe and you can see the wood surface."

The three bathrooms had to be decluttered of bottles and jars, which were stored out of sight in vanities and cupboards. Repairs also had to be made in the family bathroom. A few tiles behind the toilet had to be replaced. Since these couldn't be

Tomasz Majcherczyk

Far Left: The drapes, hung wide and high of the frame, emphasize the size of the window, while minimizing the large dining table that once threatened to dwarf the room.

Left: The recently renovated and decorated boys bedroom only needed a decluttering, and some rearranging. Notice how Bruno balanced palette and weight in the room, though: blue bedspreads in the centre, green chair on one side, green armoire on the other; descending stacked items on the armoire, the lower height dresser, and the chair cushions.

Right: Get extra pillows—not just queen size but king size as well, even for a queen bed so that the kings are backdrop for the smaller queen size. The big pillows and mix of colours—or straight neutrals—makes it look like a hotel suite. And beds are a visual thing.

matched exactly to the other tiles, Bruno decided to paint the lower part of the tiled wall in white.

In the basement, where low ceilings automatically increase a cramped feel, Bruno decluttered the fireplace area and returned it to a working fireplace. He recommends steam-cleaning carpets—but if a carpet really smells, replace it because "there are some smells, like dampness, you just can't rid of." In this case, there were good hardwood floors in the basement, but the area carpet—easy enough to remove—was a little musty, so Bruno purchased a jute carpet (from IKEA) which warmed up the space, and added a nice smell of fresh-mown grass.

Next, Bruno tackled paint touch-ups and minor repairs. Since the overall palette was soft, there was no need for a major repainting, but the walls needed washing. "I tend not to touch the walls if they're in neutral colours and there's no damage," Bruno says. If painting is necessary, he'll choose paler colours like off white, various yellows, grey and putty, which are sufficient to highlight white trim without standing out too much.

Some of the door trim had been nicked, so it needed painting. "If trim, moulding, quarter round

are all dinged up, a room can look disjointed. But paint it, and all of a sudden the line is crisp and the floor looks straight."

In the kitchen, walls were in good shape, cabinetry was quite new, and the black and white ceramic tile floor was immaculate. But there was a bit of window damage that needed repair, followed by painting a portion of the room by the window.

With the cleaning, painting and repairs complete, Bruno tackled the furniture rearranging. Staging, he believes, is just "one step to the side of decorating." He tries to look at a house the way a buyer would, that is, can I see myself living here and will my furniture fit? For Bruno, that means each room needs to have an identity and function, and needs to feel spacious.

But he also tries to look at a house in terms of straight decorating. In fact, the homeowners wished they'd call him earlier—though they wouldn't likely have changed their minds about moving, since they needed the extra space, but they would have enjoyed their home while living in it, Bruno says. "Once I was finished, they were surprised to find they had a lovely living and dining room, that they could have entertained with other families—especially once the basement was made more habitable for kids."

It's hard to articulate the magic that happens with rearranging. In some ways it's instinctive, but there are certain principles, Bruno says. "Certain combos you put together are always right—two couches facing each other, one couch facing two chairs."

Tomasz Majcherczyk

In general, there are certain classic configurations for a living room, especially when you have a fireplace. All you need is a nice piece of carpet, sofa and chairs, and enough lamps! When there's no fireplace, he suggests substituting an armoire.

One mistake most people make when arranging furniture is to place it all against the wall, assuming that will make the room look larger. In actual fact, pulling furniture closer to the centre of the room creates the illusion of more space. There's also a perception that the home is easier to clean when you can see expanses of floor.

As for how many pieces, Bruno finds that most rooms need just one or two larger pieces as anchors. In the living room, these were the armoire, couch and fireplace. Once those are in place, he "sprinkles" smaller, lighter pieces throughout—chairs with light upholstery, small coffee and end tables.

Items with legs are preferable, so that carpets or wood floors can be seen; even ottomans are better with legs than having that dead weight in the middle of the room. He removes large bulky chairs, or items that sit too low to the ground, for that reason.

Thankfully, the homeowners had a lot of good furniture—and family and friends willing to lend what they didn't have, so there was no need to rent.

The final touches were accessories, some of which were borrowed. Artwork, which adds a

Below: The two sofas in a wide pinstripe blue and white fabric were there already, and all they needed was a steam cleaning. An old wooden chest serves as a coffee table, a jute rug (from IKEA) covers the hardwood and adds much needed warmth. The 1930s moveable bar was turned to face the wall, creating an unobtrusive console that also provided storage. Several lamps combat the natural darkness of the basement, and simple blue drapery panels soften the length of the one wall. With the fireplace now working, the basement became a room the kids and parents could use—a place for family movie night, or when company is over for the kids to retreat to for movies or video games.

lot to a space, came from friends and family. Two perfect side chairs to add to the dining room were located in the garage, and chafing dishes and silver candlesticks came out of hiding from drawers and cupboards. Bruno cautions against bringing out too many accessories, though, because "it can feel contrived and sometimes too personal, and people also enjoy seeing some wall and table space."

What's missing afterward is purchased, and usually from discount or big box stores. Bruno will purchase soft furnishings—curtains, sheets, pillows, slipcovers. "These are the things people rarely get around to, or don't buy frequently, and these are the details that finish a room so well."

Curtains were used to great effect in the dining room. Adding linen drapery panels (from IKEA) at the extreme edge of the window and above the frame, gave the window much grander proportions, which then minimized the size of the huge dining

table. "The drapery increased the window from four feet wide to six feet wide," says Bruno. "Before the table dwarfed the room and the window looked tiny, and now it's the reverse."

In the living room, paper blinds that look like fabric provided luminosity and privacy, while putty linen drapes framed the window. For the kitchen, Bruno chose a simple white Roman blind that gave the bay window a finishing touch.

Curtains saved the day in the basement, too. The two windows on the eight-foot long wall were small and high up, but when blue drapery panels were hung on either side of each window, it softened the wall and gave the appearance that the window stretched the entire length of the wall.

Bruno admits he has a weakness for lamps because lots of light and curtains will make a home look finished and high end. If you take away those things, it doesn't matter how nice the furniture,

Tomasz Majcherczyk

Below: Since the living room sofa was dated with its pink and grey upholstery, but the shape was pleasing, Bruno found the perfect stretchy camel coloured slipcover at Walmart. After fitting it snugly around the sofa, and adding two silk cushions, it looked new. An artful vignette with two leggy caneback chairs and a small table could have been placed on either side of the fireplace to make more room, but the lightness of the furniture allowed for visibility through it to other parts of the room, and into adjoining spaces, enhancing the sense of space.

the home will look empty. So he buys lots of lamps when staging—especially boxed sets from stores like Walmart where you can get inexpensive classic reproductions which look good in both contemporary and traditional spaces.

Bruno believes the average room should have four to six lamps. "Light adds life to a room immediately, and gives the sense that people spend time in there, even if it's never used. You may only barely see them, but the glow of a lamp seen from outside, during the day or night is really inviting," Bruno says. "And inside, pools of light make a room seem larger, and spreads warmth, making a room more inviting, creating great shadows, highlighting certain objects and even changing and softening the wall colour. And the beautiful thing is, light takes up no space, but creates lots of it."

In the dining room, after the buffet was cleared, he positioned two of these lamps on either side of a large blue willow container. "The lamps really help light up the wood table, introduces some twinkle

Tomasz Majcherczyk

Below: What makes a room or home look large is being able to see through it. Here, you can see from the front hall through the kitchen to the back yard. "Those glimpses, even if the depth behind them is tiny, enlarge the spatial sense," Bruno finds. "It feels as though the house goes beyond its own borders, because the mind makes up the missing information."

and reflection, and the sparkle helps a room look really clean," Bruno says.

Bruno's Tips

· Lamps for sure—on the mantel, the tables, the floor. They don't have to match exactly but the shades should be more or less the same. Boxed sets are perfect, because they're already matched, and it's easy to find classic shapes that go well with both contemporary and traditional styles.
· Keep carpets as neutral as possible and have

them in the living room and family room, but not necessarily in the dining room. If you can manage it financially, splurge on carpets. The most important aspect is the size—it should be large enough that furniture can fit on it, not off.
· Curtains finish a room properly, make a room look larger and create a focal point at the window. Drape panels on either side of the window frame in double thickness. If the window is small, you can do one panel on each side, a larger window will need more panels. You need one panel for every

Tomasz Majcherczyk

24-inches of window space, even if the package says it covers 50-inches. Even if you're not closing them, it's nice to have the thickness. When curtains are not closed, add a sheer to hang between the panels—it's very European looking and offers diffused light and privacy. A large window is also a great backdrop for furniture—two chairs, a small side table and a lamp, for example.

· Armoires and china cabinets are great for both display and concealment. This house didn't have a proper main floor family room, although the basement took a lot of the overflow, so the living room armoire handled storage of games, toys, puzzles and audio-video equipment.

· Choose small tables in living and family rooms, as opposed to a large coffee table, because it keeps the space open, makes visible the expanse of floor and are more easily moved when necessary.

· Paint only if the walls are in a strong or heavy colour, or if paint is badly worn and can't be scrubbed clean. If walls haven't been painted for several years, cleaning can only go so far—if you scrub walls too hard, even with mild soapy water, you can take some of the paint off.

· Don't go too far with house dressing, because you run the risk of the home becoming too personal. Your aim is to make the décor foolproof, so that people have a general idea of how to work the space, but not so contrived that they feel they could never accomplish what you've done.

· Don't hesitate to buy new bedlinens. You can pick up a great contemporary duvet set for very little money, and it spruces up the bedroom tremendously.

GO WITH THE FLOW
Stager Nora Lukss celebrates, rather than fights, this modern home's features

Housing Type

Moderate to highly priced, multi-level detached brick home in the family-oriented Beach neighbourhood of Toronto.

Selling History

Nora and Al had lived in this home for about 13 years, and had from time to time put it up for sale to test the market. Nora kept it scrupulously clean but had never actually staged it.

When the couple decided on a major lifestyle change—moving to a southern locale—Nora began implementing upgrades. The basement got a new powder room, carpeting, laundry facilities, an office for Nora and a guest bedroom.

Nora and Al were ready to list by winter 2006, and their agent made some staging suggestions based on what he perceived the market to be—families wanting three-bedroom homes. Nora carried out the agent's suggestions, although she

felt they weren't entirely appropriate for the house, and that the list price was a bit high. When it didn't sell in a brisk market (and the three offers they had fell through), they pulled it off the market. "Our biggest mistake," Nora says, "was our choice of agent."

They hired another agent, Diane Chaput, feeling that she "got" their house—a modern multilevel light and airy brick home in a traditional Beach neighbourhood of Craftsmen cottages, Victorian frames and 1940s bungalows.

Nora agreed with Chaput's assessment that making the house into something it wasn't—a cozy two-storey traditional family home—would never fly. They emphasised the modern beauty of high ceilings, big windows, natural light and different levels, and ratcheted up the appeal for potential buyers more like Al and Nora—a childless couple with two busy careers.

Chaput's suggestions included expanding

Steve Leach

entertainment areas, going back to two full home offices (and one small office nook), reducing bedrooms from three to two, switching functions in two main space areas, and making over the back yard into a chic "outdoor room" for lounging and entertaining.

The house was listed at $699K and sold in 10 days at asking price.

Stager

Nora Lukss is both homeowner and stager. She completed an interior design program in 2003 and has been doing a range of commercial and residential projects. Her staging credits include her home plus those of a few friends.

Features

This relatively new home was built by an architect and had many luxury finishes. The home boasted large principal rooms and had lots of light.

Deficiency List

· Previous list price was a little high.
· Access from the kitchen to the back yard was not capitalized on.
· The master bath had dark navy blue tiles.
· Large master, but small extra bedrooms.
· Drab, unkempt, uninviting back yard; to the prospective buyer, Nora believes it looked like a lot of work, and that's just what busy professionals don't want—more work. It also stood in stark contrast to the rest of the house, which was sleek, modern, turnkey.

What Nora Did

Rather than stage their bedroom plus two other small "children's" bedrooms upstairs, Nora took out the rental furniture she had (dark brown furniture in the master, and children's beds and dressers in the other two rooms) and turned one of the small bedrooms back into an office. The guest bedroom in the basement was turned back into the large home office it had originally been for Al.

Nora moved the den, which she and Al had always enjoyed for relaxing and cooking dinner together, into the upstairs living area and brought in the glass dining table and chairs.

She removed all greenery from the upper-level living room—the agent felt it was important to reveal the lovely architectural bones of the home, and plants obscured those. She also removed some of the older furniture from the living room, and added the modern classic furniture from the den (a white Ultrasuede sofa, Le Corbusier–style lounger and chair, leather ottoman, white shaggy carpet); the one colour-blocked wall was repainted a pale blue.

The master bath had a high-contrast scheme of dark blue tiles and white grout—with white fixtures and an old melamine double vanity with a wall-to-wall mirror above it. Nora knew that ripping out the tiles was out of the question short of blasting them out, so she decided to work around them. She chose a bathroom spa as her conceptual starting point, which generated visions of water, big white fluffy towels and an organic component of some kind. After the transformation, the space felt fresh and crisp, yet tranquil.

"I knew the grout lines would be a problem so to minimize them, I added even more white into the space," Nora recalls. "First off, I cleaned them so they sparkled. Then I added new stainless steel towel holders, on which I hung four big thirsty towels, which in themselves covered up a lot of the blue tiles. A big white fluffy bath mat covered a large part of the floor. To ground the blue tiles and make the white elements pop out, I hired my carpenter to create four new doors for the vanity, two frames for two mirrors and a simple shelf, all made of birch and stained a chocolate brown colour. The wood also enhanced the natural feeling I was aiming for, which was further developed with organic textured baskets filled with small white towels. Blue glass vases echoed the blue tiles, and a white silk flower in each corresponded nicely with the white spa items."

The two mirrors over the vanity gave the impression of two washing stations. On the brown wood shelf above the toilet, three rolls of white paper and a white vessel with aloe reinforced the organic feel. The brown, white and blue scheme was carried through to the master bedroom, so the two rooms would flow together.

The largest change was the creation of an outdoor living space in the back yard. After measuring the space, and producing an AutoCAD drawing including the items that had to remain—the triangular deck, fences, partial brick wall and interlocking stone path—Nora was left with a long

Photos by Steve Leach

narrow rectangle and an imposing brick wall to the south.

To give the impression of a lot of space, she created three separate zones—the triangular deck, large, uncluttered and perfect for summer cocktails; an awning-covered dining area with large natural stone pavers, a table and four chairs; and a small sunning/reading zone with two teak loungers and a side table. This last zone was directly in line with the kitchen, in order to draw the eye outward to the end boundary of the yard, increasing the visual space.

To reinforce the concept, Nora added outdoor lighting, which was hidden behind three tall potted plants to give height and texture to this farthest focal point. To reinforce the three different areas, Nora changed the "floor" material: zone 1 was wood decking and was connected to zone 2 by a gravel path. Zone 2, a dining area on a floor of large natural stone tiles, was connected by a gravel path to zone 3, which sat on a floor of cedar mulch to evoke a natural setting.

Nora's Tips

· Staging isn't always the best way a family functions. Originally we had the dining room a half level up from the kitchen, where the living room was. Al and I spent most of our time in the kitchen/den, preparing meals, relaxing, watching TV together—it was the most used communal space. When friends came over, we'd take dinner up to the large living and dining area.

Steve Leach

· Assumptions are funny things. In my first staging plan, I had believed that the potential buyers in the neighbourhood would be young families, where it's usually the mom preparing meals, and wanting to watch over children playing in the den or in the back yard. But the sale proved that a house will attract the buyers meant for it—in our case a childless career-oriented couple very much like ourselves. So the lesson is, you should stage for yourself as long as you abide by a few design principles—clearly defined focus for each space, and cover all the needs (food prep, entertaining, sleeping and so on).

· The back yard makeover was a major component of the staging—the number of zones implied lots of space, and the focal point at the end of the yard created by the height, texture and visual interest implied length.

· Shop carefully—the new owners loved the table, chairs and awning I picked up at end-of-season sales at various big box stores so much, they asked to buy the entire set along with the house.

PART 3 *The Processes*

Tomasz Majcherczyk

GETTING A LIFE
Heather Shaw stages an empty home

Housing Type
Detached brick, 1920s, standard two-storey in north Toronto.

Selling History
The homeowner bought this home in 2005 for her family to live in while she was renovating their own family home. When it was done, she and the family had moved in, she renovated the main floor of this house, putting in a new kitchen, powder room and hardwood throughout. She then painted the whole main floor a smooth pecan cream.

But there was no furniture, accessories or art, so Heather was called 10 days before the house was listed. She pointed out small repairs that needed to be done, developed a master plan for furnishings and then styled over two days.

The house sold for $850K in one week, $31k over asking.

The Stager
Heather Shaw came to staging via a circuitous route. As a TV and film accountant, she was organized and fast, and had an eye for business—and good deals. She and her family zig-zagged their way up the housing ladder, moving every few years and fixing, staging and selling as they went. At the sale of her last house, the agents all clamoured to know who staged it, especially when the house sold for an astronomical amount over asking, commanding the highest price in that area's selling history.

When the vendor of this 1920s brick house hired Astrid Willemson as her agent, Astrid immediately called Heather.

Features
· beautiful new kitchen and powder room
· new hardwood
· lots of space on the main floor—space for a formal

living room, a dining room open to the new family room, and even a small nook for a home office setup

· lots of light, and easy access to the back yard

Less than lovely features

· unrenovated second floor
· bathroom in good shape, but a little dated
· small bedrooms with tiny closets
· unrenovated basement

What Heather Did

Heather's game plan was to give emphasis to the main floor, and outfit the upstairs with furnished bedrooms, and make it cheerful. The basement,

though unrenovated, benefited from a fresh coat of white paint, and an area carpet sized to fit.

Day One: Before Heather drew up a furniture list, she compiled a must-do deficiency list, which included finishing the fireplace mantel, vents on the family room fireplace and fixture plates. There was also one lone wire—an obsolete part of the deleted heating system that had never been removed—coming out of the wall. It required removing, and the wall patched and painted. "You don't want anything visually distracting," says Heather, "because buyers obsess on small things—they'd focus on the loose wire rather than on the gorgeous new kitchen. Plus you want to sell

Tomasz Majcherczyk

a house that's as low maintenance as possible—that means no loose ends. Literally."

Heather mentally configured the space to accommodate a great room, a generous dining room, a streamlined living room and three good-sized bedrooms, with a sunroom/home office off the master bedroom.

She then worked out with Astrid, the agent, how detailed the staging would be. For example, the house had no window treatments. "I didn't think it necessary to add any," Heather says, "because the house had so much light and great views. Besides, having drapery made is expensive." The agent agreed.

Since the house had to be ready in less than two weeks, Heather called in trades right away to delete the obsolete wire, drywall the basement ceiling and paint the entire basement.

Day 2: While the trades were busy completing repairs (which took 8 days), Heather was developing a furniture plan. Regardless of the kind of space—filled or empty—she says it's critical to develop a whole house plan, envisioning how to best use the space and then present it that way.

After measuring the rooms and drawing up a rough floor plan of the house, Heather went "shopping" for furniture in three houses—her own, Astrid's and the homeowner's.

The homeowner had the perfect pair of ivory

Tomasz Majcherczyk

Tomasz Majcherczyk

chenille loveseats, dining table, mirror, a queen-size wooden bed frame and a white-painted wooden single bed. Heather had dining chairs, carpets, a coffee table and side table. Astrid contributed floor lamps for the living room and table lamps in the family room, plus the desk between the dining area and family grouping. The artwork was a collective effort from all three. The sectional, purchased by the homeowner for her other home, fit perfectly in the family room, making the space look more uniform. Fortunately, it matched the walls.

The large area rug for the basement came from the homeowner, who instructed Heather to cut it to fit the room because that was a less expensive option than installing $3,000 worth of wall-to-wall carpet.

For the bedrooms, Heather has a full inventory of bedding. She claims to have a bedsheet addiction, and owns enough to "pretty much match any room." And if she doesn't have a match, "there's always white," she adds.

Heather arranged for vans to pick up furniture and accessories at the various locations and deliver them to the house.

Day 3: The moving van arrived with its first load of furniture and accessories. Heather directed where each piece was to go. Once the furniture was unloaded, Heather and her assistant got to work moving it into its exact place.

While Heather arranged the living room, Andrea set up and ironed the sectional in the family room. By the end of the day, all the furniture was in place, most of the arranging of accessories done, and artwork placed against the walls ready for hanging the next day.

The rug in the children's bedroom had to be stretched out, upside down, with heavy objects on top to stop it curling from being stored too long rolled up.

A thick terry shower curtain was hung in the grey marble bathroom, simple white towels folded and candles added to the counter.

The carpet for the basement had to be sized and rolled under rather than cut. The lovely celadon-

Tomasz Majcherczyk

and-tan plaid sofa, which Heather thought would be perfect for the basement, wouldn't fit down the stairs no matter how hard they tried. It had to be returned to Heather's house.

Day 4: Finishing Touches. The elegant French dining table got a simple centrepiece of four pillar candles in glass; an Oriental runner was placed under the table, with little worry about the fact that it was nowhere near wide enough to place chairs on—it just enhances the French flair and ambience. Four white chairs, which contrasted with the burnished maple of the table, were pulled up to the table, and a large square mirror was placed on the floor, leaning against the wall to help expand the space visually by bringing in more light and sparkle.

A home office was created using a large antique desk and chair placed next to the family room fireplace. It even had a view—the backward glimpse as seen through the large square mirror that leans against the wall next to it.

The family room was simple—the large tan sectional, a square red Persian carpet, round end table, and closer to the fireplace, a pair of leggy slipper chairs. A bushy faux tree filled out the corner behind one of the chairs.

The living room was laid out on a symmetrical plan—the fireplace flanked by two simple floor lamps, and two ivory loveseats facing each other over an ebony tray table. A red Aubusson carpet (from Heather's stash) pulled the room's grouping together, while three framed lithographs lined the mantel. An antique secretary filled one corner of the room, its book-lined shelves adding a homey touch.

The basement—*sans* sofa—was what it was—a large space with carpeting, casual Le Corbusier lounge chairs and an oversize Andy Warhol poster.

Upstairs, the bedrooms came together nicely. With just the right brushstrokes, Heather filled the blank canvas of the house. An Oriental carpet and Arts and Crafts desk and chair created a sunny home office attached to the master bedroom, where the Arts and Crafts theme continued: a wooden bed, 1920s glass-front bookcase, and brown-and-white bedding punched up by red accents and another reddish-hued Oriental carpet.

Tomasz Majcherczyk

Below: Heather's ingenuity shows in this dining area—rather than be daunted by not having a full size carpet, she placed an oriental runner under the table just to give the area a little lift. She also mixed white painted chairs with a gorgeous high-sheen antique French table.

One child's room was given a cheery blue, yellow and green theme. A three-quarter bed and dresser—white-painted wood in the shabby chic style—were freshened and brightened with blue, yellow and green bedcovers.

The other child's room revealed a modern twist on the twin set, with two beds dressed in pink with brown polka dots. A white-painted side table served both beds, and a fresh pot of tulips brought a little of the outdoors in. The white headboards were borrowed from Astrid.

Day 5: Agent's open house.

The response of agents at the open house was unanimous. "Everyone loved it," Astrid Willemson, the agent for the home, says. "Most couldn't believe the transition from what it was. The agent who listed it the first time a couple of years before was in shock. They couldn't believe how it went from a tired 80s house to this modern, light-filled spacious family home that's also perfect for entertaining."

Although the new kitchen had a lot to do with the feeling of space and good energy the other

Tomasz Majcherczyk

Top: New bed linens make all the difference in staging a bedroom, especially when the house has been empty like this one. Here, a girls room is fresh and pretty in brown and pink.

Bottom: It's hard to go wrong with a white backdrop—any colour goes with it. White paint on old furniture also hides a multitude of sins.

Tomasz Majcherczyk

Tomasz Majcherczyk

major difference was the furnishings and their placement. "You didn't get stuck walking around and you didn't feel closed in," Astrid recalls.

It felt so good, the agents were practically lined up with their checkbooks open. Listed on a Wednesday, shown at the agents' open house on a Thursday, the offers came flying in right away. Astrid refused them all, waiting until the following Tuesday to accept any offers, and the house sold the same evening.

Heather's Tips

· If something is a can of worms, don't put a plant in front of it in hopes that no one will notice—fix it!
· Be careful of generic accessories—in a high-end home, you have buyers who are quite conscious of product quality. Don't install Home Depot lights; head to a higher-end lighting supplier for them instead.
· You don't need a lot of accessories to make an empty home feel lived in. You just need to have real accessories—less matchy stuff and more realistic, eclectic items.
· We all have mystery things we inherit with a house, but homeowners are scared off by the prospect of potential work. Minimize those fears—the more you provide as done the less they will have to do.
· A lot of staging is combatting the feeling of "I have to do that, and why is that off."
· Heather says the difference between staging your home and designing it is time, budget and stress levels. "Staging is very fast—you're not going down to Primavera and ordering the perfect fabric, but heading to Winners for pillows. And you're not looking for the perfect couch or the perfect light, but items that will work well together. We changed the light fixtures at Kimbark/Julia's, but I wasn't looking for the perfect chandelier. And I found an appropriate, well-priced high-end chandelier on sale at Universal Lighting, a Toronto lighting store.
· Don't try to go antiseptic, and depersonalize totally; if the house shows that you have loved living here, that means you've cleaned it, decorated it, fixed it, and all the buyer has to do is move his or her stuff in and continue being happy here. So don't get rid of all the family photos—most people love beautiful pictures of smiling kids—just pare down a little.
· Make sure your home telegraphs happiness through its use of colour, details and accessories. Heather has a lot of red in her "kit bag" because it goes with so much—blues, greens, chocolate brown.
· Make sure that (for the most part) three people can comfortably move around the space, without anyone having to wait for anyone else. No buyer should go home after seeing your house with hip bruises.
· Make sure it's possible to look out every window, because everyone wants a glimpse of the outside, up close.
· For very little money, you can send your washed bed linens to the dry cleaners and they come back crisply ironed.

THE DREAM TEAM

Joy and Cesare Verde, and Julia Hall tame the clutter

The House

Small detached home in a desirable neighbourhood.

Selling History

The owner purchased this home four years ago because it was in a kid-friendly neighbourhood she believed would benefit her daughter. But when she visited friends in her original stomping grounds on the other side of the city and stumbled upon a house she fell in love with, she called Joy.

While the market was fairly brisk, and the house had some nice features, like a new kitchen and bathroom, it was small. Rather than list too high and risk no takers, Joy listed it at $550K and it sold within a few days for $562K.

Stagers: The Dream Team

Joy Verde is a Toronto real estate agent who stages her clients' homes as part of her sales package. She believes in being honest about a house. "Prepare or beware" is her rallying cry—prepare the house properly, or beware of it sitting with no offers.

Staging should maximize the home's potential, Verde believes, without going overboard. That's one reason why Verde's dream team—husband Cesare and decorator Julia Hall—uses as much of the vendor's furnishings as possible.

Joy went over with the homeowner what needed to be done to bring the house to its peak form. "We're selling space, perspective and lifestyle," Joy says. But you need to study the market, be out looking at product all the time, and know what needs to be done in what location. "Otherwise, you're comparing apples to oranges."

Joy then sent in a house inspector, to check what repairs needed doing. He came with his metal detector looking for buried oil tanks, checked out the furnace, roof, joists, mechanical systems and whether there was any termite activity. "He's tough," Joy admits. "But my motto is always: disclose, disclose, disclose."

Joy also felt the dining and living rooms should be flipped. "Flow and light are really important factors. Having the living room straight ahead as you walk in the front door made more sense than around the corner. And it was where you look out the window at the back yard."

Because the neighbourhood was family oriented—good schools, nice safe parks—Joy felt the dark basement needed attention. It would make a great playroom, but not without a serious declutter, a fresh coat of paint and new carpeting. She also felt that the third bedroom needed to return to its original use, though keeping the small wood desk and a laptop wouldn't overly confuse its function.

The window washer was sent in. "My trade secret? Nothing sells a house like clean windows."

Another of her pet peeves is mouldy or cracked caulking: "It screams out the house hasn't been cared for."

Here's an overview of Joy's game plan:

Monday: painters
Tuesday 9:15 am: termite inspection
Wednesday 1 pm: home inspection
Wednesday: pack and move excess items to storage, toys to goodwill, etc.
Thursday 11-12: window cleaners
Thursday and Friday: staging
Sunday or Monday: cleaning person and final prep
Monday: photos
Wednesday: agents' open house
Saturday/Sunday: public open house
Monday evening: Take offers

Once Joy figured out how the house was to be presented overall, and the house inspection and repairs were finished, Cesare and Julia took a pre-inspection and mentally noted what they would do to stage the home.

Julia and Cesare quickly assessed the house in their heads. They delegated the decluttering to the homeowner, contracted out the painting and

Tomasz Majcherczyk

arranged for cleaners. On styling day, they showed up with their collective creative brains—and their muscles.

As it turned out, Julia and Cesare worked solidly for 14 hours, spread out over two or three days, moving furniture, hanging pictures and arranging accessories.

Day 1: Painters arrive, move furniture into the middle of the rooms that have been earmarked for painting. The master bedroom will be toned down from its original acid yellow to a soothing buttery yellow; the guest room, taken from its strong persimmon (which the homeowner was trying to match from the stained glass) to the Greenmount silk suggested by Julia, and the basement painted an overall warm light neutral.

Day 2: Cesare and Julia arrive to start moving furniture around and into the appropriate spots. Cesare says he has never seen a woman as strong as Julia—she won't wait for help to move a huge TV on her own. That's why she has good arm muscles.

Julia has never written down notes or a deficiency list on any staging jobs—she thinks about how a place should look and then brings what she needs from other rooms. She also works extremely fast. When she and her husband decided to sell their house a few years ago, she hired a nanny for her two small children, donned her running shoes and worked demon-like for a solid week. The house ended up selling for $150K more than what they'd paid for it a year earlier, in a slow market.

She dives right in to any task, and Cesare complies—getting on the job right away is important because vendors get antsy when they come home mid-transformation and see the house all topsy-turvy.

Julia and Cesare admit that they read each other's minds, and that they're both borderline obsessive-compulsive—Cesare with a "thing" about the proper height of artwork and the flow of a room, and Julia with her artistic precision for display.

Tomasz Majcherczyk

Below: In its previous incarnation, this room had living room furniture, but Joy felt the room made more sense as a dining room. Certainly, the wall colour blends better with the pine table and hutch. Even the artwork stands out more.

Once the pieces are in place—dining table, hutch, cabinet, child's desk and chair, twig pendant light, and dishes in place in the dining room—they realize there's still too much. Out goes the child's desk, chair, plus the iron crane sculpture. Julia borrows Joy and Cesare's set of Quebec pine chairs to go with the table.

Meanwhile, in the living room, Cesare moves the chair and sofa so that they are grouped and focused on the Asian armoire that houses the TV. He centres the bookshelf (snitched from the guest room/home office) on the wall perpendicular to this grouping so that there's a clear traffic route from the front door to the kitchen.

Julia brought some striped and plaid pillows for the living room, which she thought might work—they don't. But a small celadon green with a faint burgundy stripe is perfect.

Julia then asks Cesare to help her move the sofa out of the home office upstairs, so they can add the new bed. They also remove the carpet and

bring the extra bookshelf downstairs.

In the basement, things are added, but even more is taken away.

The kitchen becomes the repository for all the boxes of items not needed for the staging—and already packed up for Kate's move to her new house.

Day 3: Fun time begins. Julia and Cesare get to play with stuff. They also hunt down last-minute things that the owner has "decluttered" and tucked away out of sight—like the large round planter unearthed from the basement crawl space. It's perfect for the top of the Asian armoire. Stuck behind the bathroom curtain is the perfect French country floral for beside the bed in the guest room. It will go perfectly with a length of Pierre Frey fabric Julia picked up a few years back and plans to use for a cover on the guest room bed. For the most part, they use the homeowner's things, such as Kate's fine

Photos by Tomasz Majcherczyk

Below: The tone of the master bedroom was already set with the antique maple bed—what Julia and Cesare did was bring out more of the room's personality. The result was a toning down of some elements—acid yellow walls are now butter coloured, stuff taken off the antique night tables—and a punching up of others, like the handsome folk art steamer on top of the dresser, and the coral plaid duvet on the bed.

collection of Canadian artwork. All the team has to do is switch paintings around to show them off in a better light.

A large folk art model of a steamship is placed on top of the black dresser in the master bedroom—the new soft yellow is a good backdrop for this stunning piece. Over the bed in the master Julia hangs a French country wrought iron grate complete with dried coral and yellow roses that will match perfectly with both the coral plaid bedspread and buttery yellow walls.

Tomasz Majcherczyk

In the kitchen, Julia finds a whole set of Portmeiron china that Kate has stuffed into a cabinet, so she displays it in the glass-fronted kitchen cupboard.

Day 4: Now that the homeowner and her daughter have left for vacation, Julia and Cesare—and the cleaners—come in for one final touch-up, to make sure counters are clean and clear, appliances sparkle and displays are done. There's still the odd item a little out of place, but that's so that the house doesn't look too perfect.

Below: Hope springs eternal! Although snow covered the ground for the February showing, the porch is a haven of bright futures with cheery green and blue striped pillows on white chairs. While the buyer realizes nobody sits outside in the middle of winter, they at least know that sitting on the porch is an option at some point.

Right: Before and after—not only was the home office cluttered with papers, books and furniture, but the orange walls were blinding. Julia and Cesare pulled everything out, had the room painted buttercream, and returned only the desk to its former spot. A single bed with a beautiful Pierre Frey cover and a score of plump pillows telegraphs that this multipurpose room has style. A few artistic touches—the old French laundry hamper in the corner by the window, the whitewashed mirror frame, the tin basket of dried flowers over the bed—are just enough to bring life and movement without crowding the room all over again.

Day 5: In spite of a freak snowstorm, the turnout for the agents' open house is good. Nobody comments on the staging, which pleases Joy: "My goal in staging a house is not to bring in all this rented furniture and have the place look like a magazine spread, but to have it look real. The agents all commented on how nicely the house presented. That's a successful staging."

Joy isn't a fan of public (as opposed to agents') open houses, though. For one thing, it overexposes a house, and doesn't give the clients a chance to take the time they need with their agent. (In some areas, you can also run the risk of theft.) She does welcome clients to come through on their own, without their agent, on weekends, though.

Joy decided to list the house at $550K, although some agents thought it could be listed higher. "I wanted to be careful because of its size, and wanted to go out at a price that, if it only generated one offer, we'd be happy."

It sold for $562K.

Tomasz Majcherczyk

Below: From warehouse to playhouse: Even though the homeowner had hired an artist to paint a mural on the sliding closet doors, the space had little appeal. After removing boxes and unused items, painting the walls a warm beige, and steam cleaning the carpet, all Julia and Cesare needed to do was set up the space for fun. Leaving the central area free, because kids love to play on the floor, and adding a desk, craft table, and bookcases in a mix of antique and modern, they created a warm, inviting and colourful spot.

FURNITURE RENTAL

Google furniture rental for your hometown, and you should get several listings. In Toronto, **Dominion Furniture Rental**, www.domfurnrent.com; **Executive Furniture Rentals**, which also has a back room where you can buy retired pieces, like sofas, beds, tables, for very low prices (81 Tycos Drive, North York, 416-785-0932); **Progressive Furniture Rentals Inc.**, 25 Curity Avenue, Toronto, 416-424-3166, www.progressivefurniture.ca; **Mr. Convenience Inc.**, 3400 Pharmacy Avenue, Toronto, 416-497-2511, www.mrconvenience.com; **Easyhome**, with locations across Canada, www.easyhome.ca; **Contemporary Furniture Rentals**, 39 Jarvis Street, Toronto, 416-703-9236; **Marty Millionaire**, 345 Queen Street East, Toronto, 416-366-6433, www.martymillionaire.net.

SHOPPING

Furniture

Ballard Designs: www.ballarddesigns.com
Bombay: www.bombaycompany.com
Bombay Kids: www.bombaykids.com
Crate & Barrel: www.crateandbarrel.com
The Elegant Garage Sale: Located at 1588 Bayview Avenue, Toronto, 416-322-9744
Ethan Allen, Canada: Visit www.ethanallen.com/roomplanner to plan your rooms, or www.ethanallen.com to view their products
Faveri's Unpainted Furniture: This store has great selection and great prices! www.unpaintedfurniture.ca
IKEA: They have great classic designs and designer knock-off furniture, www.ikea.ca
Maine Cottage: www.mainecottage.com
Mitchell Gold + Bob Williams: www.mitchellgold.com
Of Things Past: www.ofthingspast.com
Pottery Barn: www.potterybarn.com

Spiegel: www.spiegel.com

Sure Fit Furniture Covers: They have stretch knit and chenille slipcovers for a snug fit, www.surefit.com

UpCountry Outlet: www.upcountry.ca

Bedding/Accessories/Draptes

The Bay: www.hbc.com

Canadian Tire: www.canadiantire.ca

Home Depot: www.homedepot.ca

HomeSense: www.homesense.ca

Linens 'n Things: Has a Nate Berkus line of interior items like lamps, etc., and a good selection of bedding, chairs, kitchen supplies, and so forth, www.canada.lnt.com

Rona: www.rona.ca

Umbra: www.umbra.ca

Walmart: www.walmart.ca

Zellers: www.hbc.com/zellers

Fabrics

BB Bargoons: They have discount fabric ends, which are great for making pillows, www.bbbargoons.com

Carole Fabrics: www.tapestria.com

Cushy Life: www.cushylife.com

designerfabricsonline.com: www.designerfabricsonline.com

Fabric Clearance Centre: www.fabricclearance.com

fabricgallery.com: www.fabricgallery.com

Fabricland: www.fabricland.com

findafabric.com: www.findafabric.com

Robert Allen: They have great colour and swatch collections, www.robertallendesign.com

F. Schumacher & Co.: www.fschumacher.com

Waverly: www.waverly.com

When visiting these websites, also look at how they dress rooms to get more staging ideas.

Storage

California Closets: www.calclosets.com

Frigo Design: They have wonderful fridge panels to update the look of your kitcen, www.frigodesign.com

Flooring

Beaulieu of America: Beaulieu carpets, with Perma Shield, guaranteed not to stain, and as durable as anything you'll ever find, www.beaulieu-usa.com

Flor: Sell modular carpet tiles so you can create your own beautiful floor carpet, www.florcatalog.com

Natural Home Rugs: Sell online seagrass carpets that are inexpensive and ship to Canada, www.naturalhomerugs.com

Pergo: Sell a variety of laminate flooring, www.pergo.com

Tech Stone: A granite look-alike that you can apply over tiles, linoleum and even outside on a deck, www.techstone.ca

Walls

WALLPAPER

Colour Your World: Has both paint and wallcoverings, and show each in room settings; they carry a variety of brands, www.colouryourworld.com

Sun Wallpaper: Has a large selection of designer wallpaper samples from manufacturers such as Stroheim & Romann, Osborne & Little, Ralph Lauren, F. Schumacher, Arthur Sanderson, William Morris & Co., Farrow & Ball, Richard E. Thibaut, Nina Campbell, Anna French, Grammercy, Carleton V, Arte, Motif and others, www.sunwallpaperandpaint.com

Wallcoverings Association: Visit this site to get information on how to shop for wallpaper, estimate quantities and properly hang wallpaper, www.wallcoverings.org

For more specific product searches, check out individual websites of wallpaper manufacturers such as Farrow and Ball (www.farrow-ball.com) or Stroheim & Romann (www.stroheim.com)

Paint

Benjamin Moore: www.benjaminmoore.ca
Glidden: www.glidden.com
paintideas.com: www.paintideas.com
Paint Quality Institute: www.paintquality.com
Sherwin-Williams: www.sherwin-williams.com

Look at the many new specialty paints: low-odour, stain-killing primers, chalkboard paint, washable paint and so on. If you have a paint chip from another line, your paint store should be able to match it.

Lighting

American Lighting Association: This site offers some good general information on lighting, www.americanlightingassoc.com

Restoration Hardware: You can get some nice, stylish lighting and hardware from this store. They often have sales, but usually only online, www.restorationhardware.com

Royal Lighting: They have a great site for finding lights and they will ship their products to customers, www.royallighting.com

Union Lighting: They have lights and more! A virtual tour online gives a hint of "what's in store," www.unionlightingandfurnishings.com

Windows

Smith+Noble: Give good ideas of what's available in window treatments, www.smithandnoble.com

You can also find drapery at Home Depot, Rona, Canadian Tire, Zellers and IKEA.

Software Programs

HomeWorks Remodelling Software CD from Home Hardware

ONLINE TO BUY

There are many online stores you can visit or purchase home furnishings from. You can often find sumptuous Frette linens at eBay and Bluefly.com. Craigslist always has furnishings at rock-bottom prices, and you can find additional great items at Target, Simply Shabby Chic, Pottery Barn and Anthropologie.

ONLINE FOR INSPIRATION

About.com: www.interiordec.about.com
Au Lit Fine Linens: www.aulitfinelinens.com
Better Homes and Gardens: www.bhg.com
Canadian House & Home: Find great articles here, www.canadianhouseandhome.com
Country Home: This is a handy site because they have ready-made palettes with all of the fabrics and colours identified, www.countryhome.com
Crate + Barrel: Visit www.crateandbarrel.com for their online catalogue
Home Portfolio: This is a great source for seeing what home design products are available, www.homeportfolio.com
House Beautiful: Has a home collection designed to mix and match for the bedroom, with 32 colours, www.housebeautifulhomecollection.com
IVillage: www.ivillage.com
Laura Ashley: www.lauraashley.com
Oprah Winfrey: She features décor from Nate Berkus, and has great accessories and display tips, www.oprah.com
Ralph Lauren Home: This is a great site for ideas, but their items are pricey, www.rlhome.polo.com
Pioneer Millworks: www.pioneermillworks.com
Recycling the Past: www.recyclingthepast.com
Southern Living: www.southernliving.com
Style at Home: www.styleathome.com
Toronto Life: This site has super shopping ideas, www.torontolife.com
Waverly: www.waverly.com

Art

Both of these sites have affordable pieces that can be shipped to Canada.
AllPosters.com: www.allposters.com
Art Select: www.artselect.com

Auctions

Ritchies: www.ritchies.com
Waddington's: www.waddingtons.ca

GENERAL HOW-TO

Bob Vila: This site will give you design tools to help you plan a room, www.bobvila.com
DIY Network: As its name suggests, this site offers lots of DIY help, www.diynetwork.com
The Home Depot: This site will give you thousands of projects, ideas and inspiration for

DIY projects, http://diy.homedepot.ca

Hometime.com: Get great how-to information at this site, www.hometime.com

See My Design: www.seemydesign.com

Smith+Noble: www.smithandnoble.com

SHOPPING TIP

Take room measurements with you. The stores—for paint, furnishings, etc.—can help you determine the right amounts, size, etc., for your job. Don't hesitate to ask for help.

THE STAGERS

Paula Whitlock

p.whitlock DESIGN

Paula has been working in design for more than a decade, first in theatre as a props and set decorator and, more recently, in residential interior design. She is an honours graduate from the International Academy of Design in Toronto, Ontario and, in 2006, created her own business p. whitlockDESIGN. Paula also has a passion for art, photography and music.

Allison Roberts

Burloak Home Staging & Design

Allison Roberts is a meticulous designer with a flair for layout, texture and colour. After graduating from Sheridan College in 2000 she opened her own design business—Burloak Home Staging & Design.

Allison's objective—in either staging to sell or designing to stay—is to showcase a home's best features and create an inviting atmosphere by working with and re-arranging a homeowner's existing furnishings, artwork and accessories.